Jean-François Bazin

Wonderful Burgundy

Photographs by Hervé Boulé

Translated by Angela Moyon

ÉDITIONS OUEST-FRANCE
13 rue du Breil, Rennes

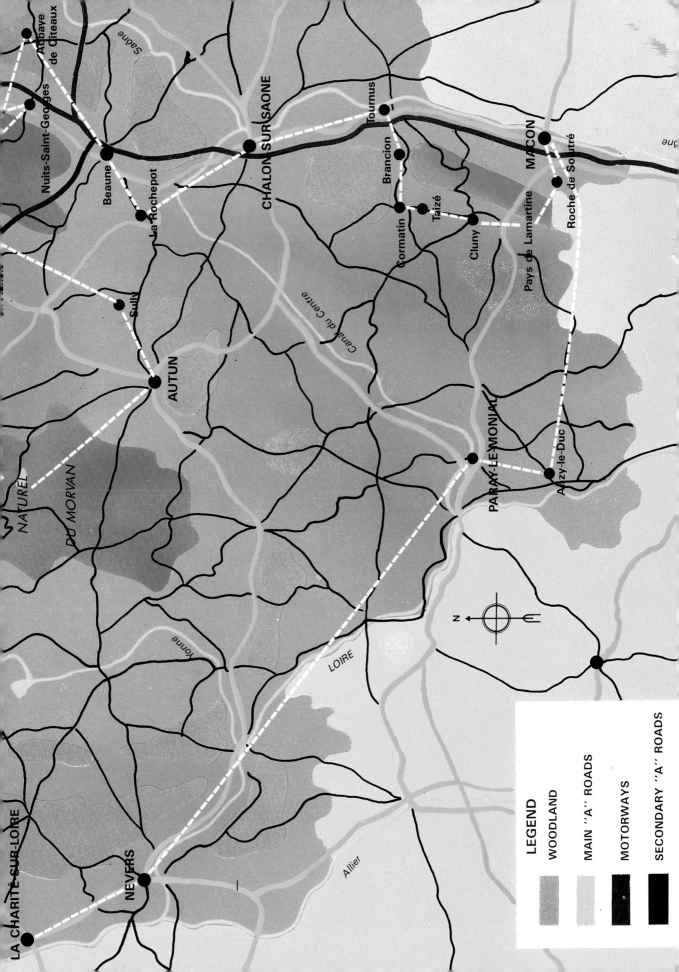

LA CHARITÉ-SUR-LOIRE

Abbaye de Cîteaux

Nuits-Saint-Georges

Saône

Beaune

La Rochepot

CHALON-SUR-SAONE

Tournus

Brancion

Cormatin

Taizé

Cluny

Pays de Lamartine

MÂCON

Roche de Solutré

Saône

Sully

AUTUN

Canal du Centre

NATUREL

DU MORVAN

PARAY-LE-MONIAL

Anzy-le-Duc

Yonne

LOIRE

N

Allier

NEVERS

LEGEND

WOODLAND

MAIN "A" ROADS

MOTORWAYS

SECONDARY "A" ROADS

The route indicated by the dotted line on the map on pages 2 and 3 indicates the order in which the places are described in the text.

The Burgundy canal near Semur-en-Auxois

Top : Vézelay.

Middle : The village and château of La Rochepot.

Bottom : The 15th- century Château de Posanges.

Front cover : The Santenay vineyard (Côtes de Beaune).
Photo : Andia. E. Cattin.

*Back cover :*The cloisters in Fontenay Abbey.

"The Burgundian's a bit hot this morning!" *exclaimed wine-growers of old as they dropped their baskets to the ground. The summer sun sparkles like the roofs of the Hospice in Beaune. Today, in the Netherlands, five centuries after the end of the reign of the Great Dukes of the Western World, a good trencherman may still hear himself told,*

"Well, you're a real Burgundian and no mistake!"

How do you become a "real Burgundian"? How can you discover and share the art and pleasure of living? The best way is to come to Burgundy. There's nothing difficult about that. But be warned. Burgundy has a snail-like character. It will not display anything to tourists in a hurry who jostle their way through the region without taking time to stop or even take breath. The region will merely shut itself away in its shell. But if you know how to approach it and appreciate it to the full, Burgundy will open its heart to you.

Vézelay is not Mont Saint-Michel. Even on August 15th, you can always find a quiet shady corner beneath a pillar in the church or outside where you have an uninterrupted view of the horizon. And if it's a visit to wine cellars that you're after, you should be aware that wine-tasting is not done here at a gallop to the sound of cannon fire, ending with a box of three bottles on the way out. You have to sniff the bouquet, take a drink, and discuss what you've got in your glass. You might go from an 82 to a 76, perhaps making a detour via a 78.

No use, either, wasting time on books. You will always find a Burgundian housewife able to explain how to make gougères or eggs poached in red wine. And there is always a Burgundian able to explain how the Charles the Bold was rather stupidly eaten by wolves. With glass in hand, you can learn to distinguish between

The Hospital in Beaune.

a Latricières-Chambertin and a Mazoyères-Chambertin. And it would be a surprise indeed if, some day or other, you did not come across La Gazette, the main character from Henri Vincenot's well-known novel, Pape des Escargots, somewhere between Alésia and Mont Beuvray.

In Burgundy, nobody ever says "Ah, if only you'd come yesterday..." On the other hand, to encourage you to stay a day longer, you might well hear, "Ah, now, if only you could be here tomorrow..." For a Burgundian likes to think about the bottle he's going to open especially for you. And he will uncork it just at the right moment, neither too soon nor too late. He will leave the cook all the time she needs.

What is called "Wait and see".

Côte-d'Or, Nièvre, Saône-et-Loire, and Yonne - four départements at the four corners of the Morvan, four "counties" that are all part of the Burgundian soul and the region's diversity.

Burgundy makes sure it has enough time to enjoy life. And you will need four keys to unlock its heart and fall totally and unconditionally in love with it.

The key to the wine-cellar, the key to the attic, the key to the kitchen, and the key to the garden.

In Burgundy, the cellar is the most important place in the house. The stairs to a cellar lead straight to paradise. Chambertin, Musigny, Romanée-Conti, Clos-Vougeot, Pommard, Volnay, Meursault, Montrachet, and Chablis, all of them gems in the crown of great wines.

Burgundians adore the region's big roofs and its attics. How many great hours have been spent in History's trunks, filled with churches, castles, artistic heritage, and historical memories! The Solutré Rock, the Lady of Vix, Vercingétorix in Alésia, the Bur-

Grotte d'Arcy-sur-Cure, in Yonne. *(Photo R. Delon Castelet.)*

gundians' Epic, the candles lit in Cluny and Cîteaux, the golden century of the Great Dukes who transformed Europe into a glittering procession during the days of the Golden Fleece.

No, you do not go down to the kitchen. You go up to it. Burgundy's genius has developed in thousands of ways, but none greater than over its cooking ranges. Burgundians have been civilised for many a long year; they have left far behind them raw meat and meat grilled over a wood fire.

They know that you can't have lunch in twenty minutes and that, among all the arts of the table, the art of conversation is one of the most precious. It is over the lunch table that you can really get to know Burgundy, a region that is decidedly up to the mark where food is concerned - poultry from Bresse, fish from the rivers Saône and Loire, the blue-blooded Charolais beef cattle …. Here, people quite naturally have a "healthy" appetite.

After lunch, it's time for the garden. "And if you arrive in my area on a summer's day, then in the bottom of a garden that I know, a garden black with shrubs and devoid of flowers, if you watched a blue tinge in the distance spreading over a round mountain where the stones, butterflies and thistles take on the same dusty bluish purple hue, you will forget all about me and you will sit there, motionless to the end of your days…" You have to admit that having the French writer Colette as your tour guide in Puisaye is quite something.

And what about Lamartine in

The delightful Romanesque church in La Rochepot.

the Mâcon region : "On the cleft threshold of three stone steps, chance has planted the roots of an ivy..."

There are a thousand and one gardens in Burgundy, some of them open to the public, others secret. There are monks' and priests' gardens, castle grounds and gardens round lock keepers' cottages. And nature is varied and constantly different as you pass from the Sénon area to the Charolais, from the Nivernais to Bresse, from the Loire Valley to the Saône Valley, from Vingeanne to the Othe region, from mountain to plain, from forest to thicket, from vineyard to rich pasture. With its ninety thousand hectares of woodland, its springs and tumbling rivers, and its deep lakes, the Morvan area at the heart of Burgundy is a great Regional Park.

You'll see, the four keys of Burgundy will unlock all the doors for you without weighing down your pockets. And what if you perhaps mix them up ? Oh really, you are impos... The rusty, almost moss-eaten one is the key to the cellar ; it is also the heaviest. The key to the attic ? It's rather like the key of G. The kitchen key is shaped vaguely like a fork and the garden key fits the quick exit from humdrum existence.

What about accommodation ? There are hotels, gîtes, bed and breakfasts, and campsites, so that is never a problem. And what if you forget your bunch of keys ? Just take the skeleton key with you.

All you have to do in Burgundy is keep your eyes and ears open, make sure you have a good appetite, and let your brain soar like a kite. Be a little in love. And then there's no doubt about it - you'll be very happy. Just like a true Burgundian.

8

Sens, the West Front of St.Stephen's Cathedral.

SENS

The Senones, a Gallic tribe, captured Rome in 390 B.C. and the reaction of the geese on the Capitol is common knowledge. The King of Sens' son, Brennus, then made the first-ever historical statement in Burgundy, "Woe betide those who are defeated!" as he threw the weight of his sword in gold coins into the ransom scales, as demanded by the Romans. The Senones are also said to have founded Galatia. Sens, which was one of the 4th Lyonnais region's major towns during the Roman Occupation, was protected

St. Stephen's Cathedral, the transept and first spans of the nave.

The south door, or Moses Door. ▶

by formidable ramparts said to be bound by golden chains. Unfortunately, these walls were demolished in the 19th century.

St. Stephen's Cathedral (Saint-Etienne) dates from the 12th and 15th centuries and is one of the finest Gothic churches anywhere in France. The revolutionaries damaged all the statues except for the one of St. Stephen (on the main door) which was cleverly given a Phrygian cap. Tombs of the Dauphin, son of Louis XV and his wife. The 237-foot high south tower houses two large bells weighing 16,000 and 14,000 kilos cast in 1560. **Cathedral treasure :** ancient fabrics, tapestries, ivory, enamel, St. Victor's shroud etc.

The **Synodal Palace** or Officiality (13th century) was damaged in 1267 when the church tower collapsed. Restoration by Viollet-le-Duc. Synodal Palace Museum and Archaeological Museum. Also worth a visit are the **Abraham House** and the **Pillar House** (16th century) in the Rue Jean Cousin.

Sens recently regrouped its museums in a wonderful set of buildings comprising the Synodal Palace, the cathedral (treasure house), the Bishop's Palace, and a number of underground chambers. This is one of the best of all Burgundy's museums.

Nearby is the former **royal Abbey of Sainte-Colombe in Saint-Denis-les-Sens** (where Thomas à Beckett lived during his exile). The church contains a reredos illustrating the "Dormition of the Virgin" (15th century). Frescoes (early 15th-century) in **Etigny** church. The author Albert Camus was killed in a car accident near Villeblevin on 4th January 1960.

Joigny on the banks of the R.Yvonne overlooked by St.Thibault's Church.

JOIGNY

Joigny, (the "Key to Burgundy") is one of History's late developers - it was not mentioned until the 10th century. Rainard the "Little Old Man" turned a monastery into a fortress then houses began to be built within the walls. The town developed further, along the banks of the R.Yonne. Today's boulevards have replaced the moat that surrounded the walls until the last century.

Marcel Aymé (1902-1967), who was born in Joigny, remembered the town in his story *Lucienne et le boucher*, but most of his work is concerned with the Jura.

Joigny was destroyed by fire in 1530 and one of its oldest districts was ravaged by an explosion in 1981. Yet the town still has some very fine 16th-century **timbered houses,** in particular the recently-restored **Rod of Jesse** and the ones on the **Place Saint-Thibault** (pottery wall covering, carvings). **Porte du Bois** (12th century). **St.John's Church** (Saint-Jean) dates from the 16th century (the 18th-century panelling in the sacristy comes from the Abbot's Residence in Vézelay). St.Madeleine-Sophie Barat, born in Joigny in 1779 and founder of the Institut du Sacré-Coeur, was christened in **St.Thi-**

bault's (16th century). She lived to see her teaching order develop in Europe, Africa and America. She died in 1865 and was canonised in 1925.

The Château de Gondi has never been completed.

Joigny has the tiny **Côte-Saint-Jacques vineyard,** the remains of a mediaeval winery. A certain Sire Leboeuf, who was a cousin of the Abbot Leboeuf famous for his history of Auxerre, attributed the happy conception of male children in Joigny to this wine! The Côte-Saint-Jacques has given its name to Michel Lorain's excellent restaurant.

SAINT-FARGEAU (Château)

This is the château used as the setting for Jean d'Ormesson's book *Au Plaisir de Dieu*. The television film based on the work was also shot in Saint-Fargeau.

The original castle was built near the R.Loing c.1000 A.D., commissioned by the son of a Bishop of Auxerre. It gave the Narbonne family a foothold in the Puisaye region. In 1255, it passed to the Bar family then, in 1450, Jacques Coeur became master of Saint-Fargeau and the Puisaye. But he soon fell from grace and although he is sometimes credited with the rebuilding of the château this is pure legend. In fact, the rebuilding (1467-1488) was the work of Antoine de Chabannes, a former companion in arms of Joan of Arc.

The place was in a very dilapidated state when Anne-Marie-Louise d'Orléans (the Grande Mademoiselle, King Louis XIV's daughter) was forced into exile in Saint-Fargeau after having taken part in the Fronde Revolt (1652-1657). She commissioned the Parisian architect François Le Vau to rebuild the château. The six towers were maintained with certain buildings and façades that were to contemporary taste. Formal grounds were laid out towards the Bourdon Lake. The château was a hive of activity. Madame de Sévigné, Turenne, and the Great Condé were all guests there at some time. As a child, the composer Lulli worked in the kitchens as a scullion.

When the Grande Mademoiselle returned to Court, she fell in love with Lauzun. There followed a further two-year period of exile in Saint-Fargeau, ordered by Louis XIV who had Lauzun imprisoned in Pignerol. The Grande Mademoiselle remained faithful to her true love, whom she eventually married and to whom she gifted her duchy of Saint-Fargeau. Then the couple broke up, but the handsome officer remained the owner of the château and its lands, which he sold in 1714 to the financier Antoine Crozat. The property then passed to the family of Michel-Robert Le Peletier des Forts, future Controller General of Finances, who kept it until 1829. A new building was erected at this time (the Fort pavilion). In 1752, fire swept through Saint-Fargeau and only the walls were left standing.

Saint-Fargeau seen from the grounds.

Saint-Fargeau, the main courtyard and its semi-circular staircase.

The château and its owners passed through the Revolution unscathed. Louis-Michel Le Peletier, known as Saint-Fargeau, belonged to the Convention and voted in favour of sending the king to the block. His murder on the following day by the guardsman Pâris made him the "first martyr of the Revolution".

In the early years of last century, the moat was drained and a landscape garden was laid out. The 19th-century interior decoration dates from the days of the Boisgelins, who preceded the d'Ormessons as owners of Saint-Fargeau.

The brick and slate château of Saint-Fargeau seems to be steeped in memories of the Grande Mademoiselle and the Le Peletier family. Its six great towers mark the corners - and pretend there are only five of them. The steps leading up to the rotunda and chapel (where Louis-Michel Le Peletier is buried) are unusually elegant. A skilful alliance of Middle Ages and the Age of Enlightenment. 100-hectare park and small lake. Open to the public 1st April to 1st November.

The château, which was in danger of being left to fall into decay, was bought in 1979 by two courageous brothers called Michel and Jacques Guyot, who have been very successful in bringing it back to life. Their main achievement is an open-air evening entertainment, staged in the summer months.

Two miles away is the **Bourdon Dam** which regulates the water supply to the Loing and Briare canals. It is a manmade lake covering an area of 220 hectares.

In **Boutissant,** in a walled 400-hectare estate that was once a 16th-century priory, is a "**wildlife park**" where stags, hinds, roe-deer, fallow-deer, and European bison roam at will (photograph hunters only).

Saint-Sauveur-en-Puisaye is filled with memories of the writer Colette.

AUXERRE

When seen from the other side of the Paul-Bert Bridge, Auxerre (pronounced "Ausserre") looks like a picture postcard. The town stands on a hilltop on the banks of the Yonne and looks rather hump-backed. Jutting up above the skyline are its towers, the Abbey Church of St.Stephen (Saint-Etienne), and the churches of St.Germain and St.Peter (Saint-Pierre).

Auxerre was a Gallic and, later, a Gallo-Roman settlement and is thought to have been converted to Christianity by St.Pélerin, who was martyred near Entrains in 304 A.D. But its most famous son was St.Germain of Auxerre, born here c.389 A.D., who was a student in Rome, sent to Auxerre as provincial governor, and appointed Bishop in 418 A.D. He fought heresy in England with St.Loup and "discovered" St.Genevieve in Nanterre. He remained famous for his ability to still stormy seas and he died in Ravenna in 448 A.D. His body was brought back to Auxerre where numerous miracles occurred.

In the latter years of the 7th century, an **abbey** was founded for the upkeep, and probably the exploitation, of this highly-prestigious tomb. In the 9th century, it was an outstanding intellectual centre accommodating 600 monks and 2,000 scholars. The crypt contains the oldest known **frescoes** in France (Carolingian period). The Romanesque belltower dates from the 12th century. Building continued on the church until the 14th century, and on the monks'

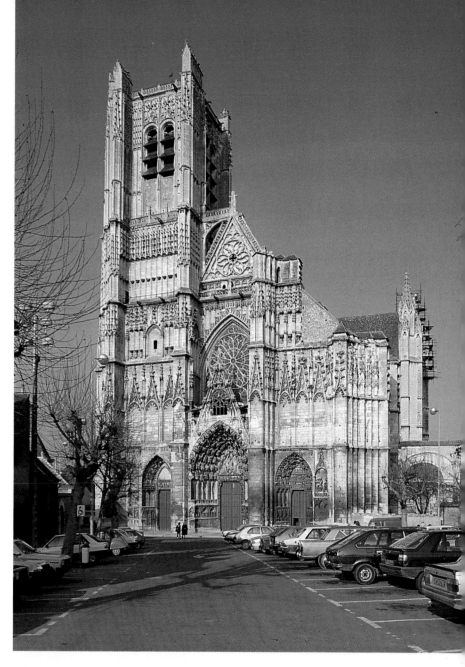

▲ The Flamboyant Gothic West Front of St.Stephen's Cathedral.

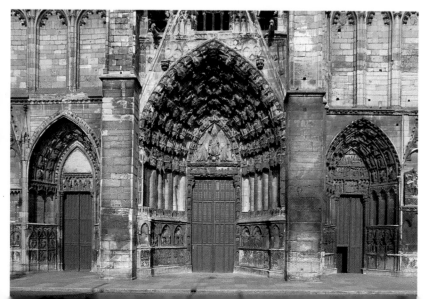

◄ The three doorways.

15

St.Stephen's Cathedral, arching on the main doorway.

◀ The Clock Tower.

lodgings until the 18th century (Abbot's residence, cloisters). St.Germain's underwent restoration in 1968.

St.Stephen's Cathedral was built over an 11th-century crypt (Romanesque fresco of "Christ on horseback"). Most of it dates from the 13th and 14th centuries, with a superb West Front in the Flamboyant Gothic style. It has 13th-century stained glass windows, a number of remarkable carvings that were badly damaged by Protestants (Noah's Ark, David and Bethsaba) and **Treasure** (gold and silverware, enamel, ivories etc.). The original design included two towers but money was short and only one was built. It was here that the Armagnac

and Burgundian factions reconciled their differences in 1412.

The **Clock Tower** dates from the 16th century and its clock from the 17th. This is the heart of the tastefully laid out pedestrian precinct. Town hall (18th century). The sculptor François Brochet carved the painted statues of Marie Noël and Cadet Roussel.

The latter was a native of Orgelet (Jura) but settled here in 1763. In 1770, he became a bailiff. Guillaume-Joseph Roussel was a ferocious patriot during the Revolution. He died, forgotten, in 1807. The knight Chenu de Souchet, wishing to poke fun at his revolutionary

fervour, wrote a few ironic verses about him, and their success far surpassed their author's hopes - Cadet Roussel became a synonym for stupidity. But it's no use looking in Auxerre for the three houses "without beams or rafters" mentioned in the song. Quite another kettle of fish was Paul Bert, born in Auxerre in 1833, an eminent physiologist and an advocate of non-church schools. As to Marie Rouget, born in 1883, she seldom left Auxerre until her death in 1968 except to go to her house in **Diges.** Under the pen name Marie Noël, she was one of the most sensitive poets of the 20th century (*La Neige qui brûle, le Cru d'Auxerre, etc.*). About as far away as you can get from the apprentice

17

The Place Saint-Nicolas in Auxerre old town.

type-setter Restif de la Bretonne!

The **Water Bus House** (Maison de la Coche d'Eau) is a reminder of the erstwhile activity of the Marine District (Art Gallery and Museum).

Leblanc-Duvernoy Museum (closed Tues., and 1st-15th Nov.) : Beauvais tapestries, furniture, glazed earthenware etc. in a fine 18th-century mansion.

The river traffic is now mainly leisure craft and cruisers.

PONTIGNY (Former Abbey)

Founded in 1114 by Hugues de Mâcon, **Pontigny Abbey** ceased to exist at the Revolution. It was a daughter-house of Cîteaux and itself created 34 abbeys or priories. In the mid 12th century, the original church was replaced by larger constructions, thanks to the generosity of Thibault le Grand, Count of Champagne. The **minster** and its side chapels look, as Abel Moreau says, like "a mother hen squatting down with her wings open to protect her chicks". Alterations were made right up until last century. Pontigny occupies an important place in the history of architecture, for it marks the transition of the Romanesque and Gothic periods.

The mighty abbey provided refuge for three Archbishops of Canterbury sent into exile after expressing opposition to the king. On the tomb of one of them, Edmund Rich (d. 1140), miracles occurred in large numbers and the Church soon acquired a certain St.Edme, canonised in 1246. Thomas à Beckett, Chancellor of England and Archbishop of Canterbury, also stayed in Pontigny.

The abbey suffered badly during the Wars of Religion. Yet during the French Revolution, St.Edme's wide following in the region spared the church. After the monks had been forced to flee, Pontigny became in turn a residence for rural missionary priests (the "Fathers of St.Edme"), a cultural centre, an Anglo-American High School, the seminary for the Mission de France (worker-priests) and a centre for the handicapped. The Mission de France is still there.

The cultural centre had a wide sphere of influence. Paul Desjardins had purchased Pontigny in 1906. As the founder of the "Union for Truth", the Parisian professor created a sort of centre for reflection which opened its doors to writers, artists and philosophers. In 1912, Joseph Bédier, André Gide, Henri Ghéon, Maurice Emmanuel and many others held discussions beneath the arbours of Pontigny. Jacques Copeau thought of settling here before going to Beaune. These were the famous "Pontigny Decades" which continued until 1939. T.S.Eliot, the author of the play *Murder in the Cathedral* which tells the story of the death of Thomas à Becket, was one of Paul Desjardins' guests.

The south aisle of the abbey church.

Overleaf: Pontigny's minster has remained intact.

CHABLIS

Chablis wine goes wonderfully well with seafood. Hardly surprising for the vines are planted on vast geological deposits of fossilised oysters (Kimeridgian Period). The vineyard follows the Serein Valley for some 13 miles - gentle valleys and hillsides usually dominated by a limestone ridge and a tuft of woodland. All the wines are white, produced from the Chardonnay grape known here as the "Beaunois".

This haute-couture wine with its sparkling freshness, crystal-green in its youth and pale yellow in its vintage, is considered to "have love in it" to use Raymond Dumay's expression. The Grands Crus cover 106 hectares. They are the "seven sages" - Bougros, Les Preuses, Grenouilles, Blanchot, Les Clos, Valmur and Vaudésir. The Premiers Crus Chablis are produced on 536 hectares covering some ten villages. The Chablis come from 1,100 hectares and 20 villages. And last but not least, the less grand lighter Chablis are produced on 116 hectares in the same area.

In an average year, the Chablis region produces 10 million bottles of wine. But on all five continents, people drink much more "fake" Chablis - it is the most misappropriated name in the world.

Chablis, the golden gate to Burgundy, was originally a monastery whose first Abbot was St.Severin, still famous as the man who cured Clovis. The **Collegiate Church of St.Martin** (1275) was one of the first churches in France to have ribbed vaulting. In 1429, Joan of Arc is said to have nailed one of her horse's shoes to the door. The **Obedientiary** contains the cave said to have housed St.Martin's relics from 877 to 887 A.D. See also St.Cosme Priory (12th century).

The **Petit-Pontigny** is a 12th-century cellar built by Cistercian monks from Pontigny. Created in 1953, the Brotherhood of the **Pillars of Chablis** holds its chapters here (4th Sunday in November).

The famous capital showing the ▶ mystical mill.

VEZELAY

This is "a boat that has dropped anchor on the skyline" according to Paul Claudel. No other place in Burgundy arouses such emotion and uplifting of the spirit. It is a "very fine act of faith".

A monastery placed under the direct authority of the Pope was founded on "Scorpion Hill" after the Vikings had destroyed the original convent founded c. 860 A.D. in Saint-Père by the Comte de Vienne, Girart de Roussillon. The relics of St.Mary Magdalen, which were discovered in Provence and whose authenticity is, of course, highly doubtful not to say totally improbable, were brought to the monastery in or shortly before the 10th century. The cult spread rapidly. Vézelay fell under Cluny's influence but the abbey stoutly retained its independence.

Built early in the 12th century, the **basilica** is, naturally enough, dedicated to St.Mary Magdalen and is called **"The Madeleine"**. The fire of 1120 (there were one thousand victims) partly destroyed it. It was rebuilt c.1130. There were 800 monks in Vézelay, the town had a population of 15,000, and occasionally up to 100,000 people slept in the huge cellars and underground passages - or in the open air. Vézelay was a mandatory stop on the road to Compostella, especially as miracles were a commonplace occurrence there.

St.Bernard preached the Second Crusade in Vézelay in 1146.

The abbey was "secularised" in 1538 when it was managed by canons under the leadership of a commendary abbot. This was the start of a long period of decline. In 1790, the

Nave and chancel of the St.Madeleine Basilica. ▶

The north aisle.

saved Vézelay - the work was to last 20 years.

Visitors should walk up the long sloping street lined with old houses leading to the Madeleine, like the 40,000 pilgrims from all over Europe who came in 1946 for the 800th anniversary of the Second Crusade. The basilica used to have two towers and two belltowers - the Protestants demolished half of them. Théodore de Bèze, Calvin's successor, was born in Vézelay.

The carvings on the tympana and capitals (some of them have been recarved) naturally draw the eye. The main doorway in the narthex (12th century) shows Christ giving the Apostles the Holy Spirit. The capitals often depict scenes from the Old Testament... or Celtic legend. The most famous carvings are the "mystical mill" (Moses is shown pouring out grain that symbolises the ancient Law), secular music, and the mortal sins. There is a Bible carved in stone.

You are sure to be surprised at the nave with its alternating white and greenish grey stone in the transverse arches, the only example of this style in Burgundy. The church is just over 400 ft. long from doorway to apse, the chancel is 114 ft. long, and the three aisles have a total width of 85 ft. while the Gothic arching is 67ft. high. Yet all these figures give little idea of the gracefulness and peace that are inspired by this great white nave. There is a Carolingian **crypt** which underwent alteration in the 13th century (reliquary of St.Mary Magdalen). At midday on the winter solstice, the light from the south-facing windows strikes the highest pillar. On the summer solstice, it strikes the absolute centre of the nave.

UNESCO has included the basilica and its surroundings in its World Heritage list. "The eternal hill", said Maurice Druon. Artists (Inghelbrecht), architects (Le Corbusier), and writers (Romain Rolland) have all lived in Vézelay. Georges Bataille, Maurice Clavel and Max-Pol Fouchet, whose civil funeral was held in this most tolerant of basilicas in 1980, all lie in graveyard here. Jules Roy wrote here. François Mitterand, who produced a particularly fine

monastery buildings were demolished. The basilica was closed. Its tower was destroyed by fire. Hens wandered in and out of the dilapidated building discovered by a dismayed Prosper Mérimée in 1834. His report drew the authorities' attention to its condition. In 1840, at the age of only 27, Viollet-le-Duc was commissioned to restore the Romanesque and Gothic building - the Romanesque nave (c.1130), Romanesque narthex (mid 12th century), Gothic transept and chancel (late 12th century, early 13th century). Although Viollet-le-Duc's work did not always meet with unanimous approval, it was praiseworthy inasmuch as it

Four capitals in the nave : the legend of St.Eugenia, the death of St.Paul the hermit, David slaying the lion, and the death of Absalon.

Overleaf : Shafts of light playing on the St.Madeleine Basilica in Vézelay.

page of writing on the subject of Vézelay, considers that the finest Alexandrine in the French language is, Vézelay, Vézelay, Vézelay, Vézelay...A homage to Aragon. Again in the graveyard is the Ysé of *Le Par-*

tage du Midi, the woman so beloved of Claudel. On her tomb, you can read "Only the rose is fragile enough to conjure up eternity".

The Christian and Yvonne Zervos Foundation conserves and displays

to the best possible advantage a large collection of modern and contemporary art bequeathed to the village of Vézelay.

Chapter house and museum in the former monks' dorter (sculptures

The wonderful central doorway in the narthex.

deposited by Viollet-le-Duc. Open June-Sept. except Tues).

The Feast of St.Madeleine is held on 22nd July.

In **Saint-Père-sous-Vézelay** is the Gallo-Roman site of **Fontaines-Salées** (Celtic sanctuary, Gallo-Roman baths etc.). 13th-15th century **church, archaeological museum** (March-Nov. except Wed. from March to Easter and from Sept. to Nov). Excellent restaurant run by Marc Meneau (l'Espérance). The attractive Cousin Valley leads back to Avallon.

NOYERS-SUR-SEREIN

Pronounced "nwhy-er", and if you can roll the "r" so much the better.

A small town that is "unique in France" according to Gaston Roupnel. It is both a historic document and a backcloth for a fancy dress parade..

Despite numerous wars, Noyers, which stands near the R.Serein, has managed to maintain its 1 round tower and 2 fortified gateways (Porte Peinte and Porte Saint-Verrotte or Porte de Pacy). Flamboyant Gothic **Notre-Dame Church** (15th century). Old streets and houses. **Town hall** (15th century with 18th century façade).

ANCY-LE-FRANC (Château)

The château of **Ancy-le-Franc** has a somewhat Italian feel about it. It was a labour of love carried out in 1544 by Antoine de Clermont, Comte de Tonnerre, grand master of the forestry commission and husband of Diane de Poitiers' sister. The building is based on designs by Serlio, the famous architect from Bologna. Did Pierre Lescot work on it? The decoration is attributed to Primaticcio.

The work continued into the 17th century. Ancy-le-Franc opened its doors to Henri IV, Louis XIII, and Louis XIV. The Marquis de Louvois, one of the Sun King's ministers, acquired the estate in 1683 and the county of Tonnerre in the following year. He had the outhouses built and commissioned Lenôtre to lay out the gardens. In 1845, the Clermont-Tonnerre family again became the owners of Ancy-le-Franc before it passed to the Mérode family. Since then, it has been purchased by a succession of owners. Unfortunately much of the furniture has been dispersed.

Although the outside is rather majestic, the inner courtyard has all the elegance of the Renaissance. The motto of the Clermont-Tonnerres, *Si omnes ego non* (All others may have denied you but I have not), is a reminder of ancient loyalty to the

Timbered houses and a fortified gateway in the heart of the mediaeval village of Noyers.

Overleaf: The elegant Château d'Ancy-le-Franc.

Burgundian Pope Calixtus II (1119-1124) during the investiture controversy, when Sibaut II de Clermont forced the Antipope Gregory VIII to leave Rome. The Clermonts originally came from the Dauphiné but settled in Burgundy when Bernardin married a Comtesse de Tonnerre.

A tour of the château always leaves pleasant memories, in particular of the charming Floral Chamber where many a visitor would enjoy spending an entire summer. The panelling, ceilings, fresoces and paintings are a constant source of surprise. Chamber of Diana. Gallery of Sacrifice.

Above : The Château de Tanlay standing proudly in the midst of a superb park.

TANLAY (Château)

The moated **château** at Tanlay is one of the finest mansions in Burgundy. It was built c.1555 for François de Coligny, lord of Andelot, who was later to make his name as joint leader of the Protestant faction with his brother, Gaspard de Coligny. François d'Andelot was a great lord, a cultivated well-read man who was a true embodiment of the spirit of the Renaissance. The League and Archive Towers, and the left-hand side of the building no doubt date from this period. In 1558, work began on the "Petit Château" at the entrance to the estate. François d'Andelot's death left the work unfinished.

The Chabots bought the "Petit Château" in 1610 and, in 1643, the Superintendant of Finances Particelli d'Hémery commissioned the architects Le Muet and Pastel to continue the work. The remainder of the château was built over the next five years, with a large park, canal, stables etc. In 1671, Tanlay was raised to a marquisate for the Secretary of State Phélypeaux de la Vrillière. The last Marquis de Tanlay, Jacques Thévenin (his family provided La Rochelle with several mayors) died in 1957.

Tanlay went down in History as one of the strongholds of Protestantism in the mid 16th century. The leaders of the faction are said to have met in the **League Tower** which has a vaulted ceiling painted with a Pompeian decor and maritime symbols that may be a reminder of the visit of Admiral de Coligny. On the upper floor, the domed roof is said to illustrate one of Ronsard's poems. The gods of Olympus are, in fact, personalities from the Court, most of them depicted in their birthday suits - Diane de Poitiers as Venus, the Duc de Guise (Mars), Admiral de Coligny (Neptune) Catherine de Medici (Juno) and the Cardinal of Lorraine (Mercury).

The **Caesar Vestibule** is decorated with busts of Roman emperors. Huge gallery decorated with trompe-l'œil.

Remains of the park. **Grand canal,** 570 yds. long. A water tower stands at one end.

The "Little Château" that leads into ▶ the park.

CHATILLON-SUR-SEINE

On the borders of Burgundy and Champagne stands Châtillon-sur-Seine, once a forward stronghold of the Duchy of Burgundy and often the scene of combat.

The **Vix Vase** is sufficient in itself to justify a visit to Châtillon-sur-Seine. It comes from a tomb containing a chariot discovered in 1953 at the foot of **Mont Lassois**, in Vix (on the Châtillon-Troyes road). **In the 6th century B.C. (the end of the Iron Age), this was the site of a mighty hillfort** which occupied a strategic position between the pewter deposits of Cornwall and Northern Italy.

The princely tomb in Vix was one of the most important archaeological finds of the present day. In the funeral chamber, intact beneath a barrow 137 ft. in diameter, René Joffroy found the body of a woman aged between 30 and 35, lying on a chariot and surrounded by precious objects, in particular a huge decorated bronze bowl. The 1,200-litre bowl was used to mix water and wine and was decorated with busts of Gorgons. It was no doubt made during the second half of the 6th century B.C. by bronzesmiths from the Greek province of Laconia (Lacedaemon-Sparta), who may perhaps have settled in Southern Italy. It is the largest Greek bronze vase known to the present day (5 ft. 4 ins. high, 4 ft. 2 ins. wide, and weighing just over 4 cwt.) It resembles the description given by Herodotes of the vase presented to Croesus, King of Lydia, by the Lacedemonians (c.550 B.C.). Another marvel is the princess's golden tiara (490 gr.) The Vix civilisation died out c.480 B.C.

The **museum** (Philandrier House, built in the Renaissance style) also contains some wonderful items unearthed during archaeological digs. The diadem of the Lady of Vix is a perfect copy. And it's just as well because - the reproduction has already been stolen once.

St.Vorles Church (11th century) built in the Early Romanesque style has connections with St.Bernard and contains a 16th-century statue of the Laying the the Tomb. Tower of the

St.Vorles' Church stands high above the Bourg district.

The famous Madonna and Child in Fontenay. ▶

castle of the Dukes of Burgundy. Château de Marmont. In the cemetery is the tomb of Maréchal Marmont, Duc de Raguze (1774-1852) who was born in Châtillon-sur-Seine. **The Douix rises here.** It is a Vauclusian spring fed by all the waters of the plateau (in dialect, a ''douix'' means the resurgence of a river) and sometimes flows at a rate of 3,000 litres a second. It runs into the R.Seine 200 yds. further on.

FONTENAY (Abbey)

This is the Cistercian abbey *par excellence*. The **former Fontenay Abbey** has not only been lovingly restored and shown off to its best advantage by its owners; its setting amidst forests and streams is a perfect evocation of the atmosphere in the monasteries of Burgundy in days gone by. "Fontenay is a wonder of the world", said Pope Innocent III. In 1981, it was included in UNESCO's world heritage list.

Fontenay is a daughter house of the Abbey of Clairvaux, itself one of the first four daughters of Cîteaux. A group of thirteen monks from Clairvaux founded the abbey in 1118, on the site of a hermitage. In 1130, the first Abbot, who was one of St. Bernard's uncles, created Fontenay on a neighbouring site. The spirit of God flows over the waters here, and the abbey's coat-of-arms is decorated with fish.

The church was consecrated on 21st September 1147 by Pope Eugene III, in the presence of ten cardinals, eight bishops, and numerous abbots, among them St. Bernard himself. The new buildings were paid for by Ebrard, former Bishop of Norwich, who retired to this spot. Henri Vincenot tells the story of the building of the abbey in his book, *Les Etoiles de Compostelle*. In the 12th century, a castle was built (it has now disappeared), as were the huge refectory and the smithy. In the 14th century, 300 monks and lay brothers lived in or near Fontenay - an abbey which had estates in, and income from 120 towns and villages. This prosperity increased until the 16th century, then fell into decline.

Overleaf: The old abbey cloisters.

The scriptorium with its ribbed vaulting.

◀ The transept of the minster.

The religious community ceased to exist on 29th October 1790, the anniversary of the founding of the abbey 672 years earlier. By then, there were only eleven people left in the vast buildings - eight monks and three servants. The property was sold and a paper mill was established in its place. Elie de Montgolfier, an industrialist from Annonay, bought it in 1820. He sold it, in turn, to his son-in-law, the engineer Marc Seguin (1786-1875) who was famous for having designed the first suspension bridge, adapted tubular boilers to locomotives, and carried out experiments in aviation. Marc Seguin was particu-

larly attentive to Fontenay's needs. He was succeeded by the Montgolfiers. The Société des Papeteries de Montbard went into liquidation in 1902. Four years later, Edouard Aynard purchased Fontenay. He was an art lover and he threw himself into the restoration of the abbey with enormous enthusiasm. He had all the factory buildings demolished so that the abbey could be seen in its original purity. The colossal enterprise was completed shortly before 1914. His descendents continued what he had started, with an unusually pleasing result.

The moving end of *Cyrano,* the film directed by Jean-Paul

Rappeneau starring Gérard Depardieu, was shot in Fontenay.

Hostelry for pilgrims and visitors Bakery (13th century). **Dovecot.** The **church** dating from 1147 is magnificent in its lack of ornamentation (13th-century statue of the Virgin Mary). The **dorter** dates from the 14th century and its rafters from the 15th century, rebuilt because of a fire. **Romanesque cloisters, chapter house and scriptorium** (where the monks used to copy and illuminate manuscripts), prison, smithy, ponds. The pavilion near the dovecot (18th century) was the residence of the commendatory abbots, who rarely set foot in Fontenay.

39

Above : The nave in the minster.

Opposite top : The dovecot, church and, on the right, the residence of the commendatory abbots.

Opposite, bottom : The cloisters, a very special place in the heart of any abbey.

Bussy-Rabutin seen from the gardens.

BUSSY-RABUTIN (Château)

The history of this château is totally overshadowed by the personality of Roger de Bussy-Rabutin who transformed a place of exile into a temple of philosophy - and insolence. Born in 1618 near Autun, and General Master of the Camp of the Light Brigade, he spent most of his war service in song and with the ladies.

During Holy Week in 1659, the rake took part in a sacrilegious drinking party and poked fun at Louis XIV's love affair with Marie Mancini. The king exiled him to his castle

in Burgundy, an old 15th- and 16th-century building partly reconstructed by François de Rabutin's grandfather in the early years of the 17th century. Bussy-Rabutin inherited the family castle and he continued its improvement, spending his forced leisure time in planning its decoration.

As a cousin of Madame de Sévigné (who repelled his advances but willingly wrote to him), the exiled Count composed literary portraits and told tales of the love affairs of the Court. The *Histoire amoureuse*

des Gaules was soon to be found clandestinely in Paris; copies were made and it was finally published. In the meantime, its author had become a member of the Académie Française. The book caused an enormous scandal. Louis XIV is said to have been amused at first. Condé, who is ill-treated in the work, then had a sequel written and falsely attributed it to Bussy-Rabutin. It was called *France galante* and it recounted the love affair of Louis XIV and Louise de la Vallière. The king immediately had the writer imprisoned in the Bastille, then ordered him to go into permanent exile in his castle in 1665. A gentleman was out in the cold!

Finding himself a country squire at the age of only 48, Bussy-Rabutin became a prolific author. He also became passionately interested in paintings that "bore witness to contemporary society" - the **Motto Chamber** (a sort of naive picture puzzle attacking the unfaithful Marquise de Montglas, interesting views of royal or princely castles); the **Chamber of the Great Warlords** (Turenne is shown as "Maréchal of France, ruler of Sedan through his wife"); the delightful **Master Bedroom** decorated with portraits of 23 high-ranking women with various virtues and paintings of Madame de Sévigné, Madame de Grignan and the unfortunate Comtesse de Bussy-Rabutin, the wife to whom he was unfaithful on their wedding night and who had to suffer the sight of the intertwined monogrammes of her husband and Madame de Montglas all over the castle; the **Golden Tower** with the "sumptuous sky above a bed for love" where there are alternating graffiti of great men (Louis XIII, Louis XIV, Mazarin, Richelieu, etc. Bussy-Rabutin himself dressed as a Roman emperor) and attractive women ("The loveliest woman of her day, less famous for her beauty than for the use to which she put it", "Lighter than air" etc.); the **Gallery of the Kings of France and the Dukes of Burgundy** completed at a later date and including Charles X.

Some of the paintings lack skill, they are often in doubtful taste, and the sense of humour may seem somewhat overdone. Yet it is all joyous and lively, and a wonderful illustration of the strange character of a rather odd person. After 17 years in exile, with occasional brief trips to Paris, the King granted Bussy-Rabutin permission to return to Court. At the age of 73, he was given a pension. At the age of 75, in 1693, he died.

Bussy-le-Grand was the birthplace, in 1771, of Andoche Junot. He was a companion in arms of Bonaparte and made Duc d'Abrantès during the capture of Portugal in 1807. General Junot died insane in 1813, in Montbard.

Bussy-Rabutin and its main courtyard.

ALESIA

Will the **Battle of Alesia** ever end ? The battle site, in Alise-Sainte-Reine, is no longer really a subject of controversy but from time to time other hypotheses raise their heads again (the most recent being La Chaux-des-Crotenays in the Jura, Guillon in Yonne). Georges Colomb, the author of *Savant Cosinus,* started the ball rolling by defending the cause of Alaise to the south of Besançon. Napoleon III committed an original sin by showing an interest in the question and having an archaeological dig carried out in Alise-Sainte-Reine. And we're now just a short step away from turning archaeology into a Bonapartist quarrel...

Mont-Auxois, the Montagne de Bussy, the Mont-Pennevelle, and the Oze and Ozerain valleys were obviously the site of the "first battle in the history of France". Designated leader of the Gauls at Bibracte (Mont-Beuvray), Vercingétorix shut himself up in the fortress, the hillfort of the Mandubians, was besieged by Julius Caesar and was forced to surrender in 52 B.C. This was one of the greatest military operations in Antiquity, for almost half a million men took part. Vercingétorix' destiny as a warlord was to last only a few months. He was taken to Rome, imprisoned for six years, and executed.

The **Gallo-Roman** town in Alésia (late 1st century B.C. - 5th century A.D.) is also very interesting. Digs are still continuing under the leadership of Joël Le Gall (the author of an excellent work on Alésia, published by Fayard) - a theatre, monument with three apses, a temple, houses, the forum, the Moritasgus sanctuary, Roman baths etc. The **Sainte-Reine Basilica**, a Merovingian church dating from the 7th century, contained the saint's relics until they were transferred to Flavigny in 865 A.D.

The great **statue of Vercingétorix** (23 ft. high), which underwent restoration a few years ago, was made by Aimé Millet and erected in 1865. The old ladies in the locality used to cross themselves as they passed,

The impressive bronze statue of Vercingétorix on the Mont Auxois.

believing the statue represented one "St.Gétorix". Viollet-le-Duc designed the base. Napoleon III updated Caesar's supposed speech to Vercingétorix, "A united Gaul, forming a single nation, moved by the same spirit, could defy the universe". The sentence might have been spoken by General de Gaulle.

Alise worships **St.Reine.** There is proof that she was martyred in Alésia in the 4th century, and in the 8th century the story of her life plagiarized St.Mary of Antioch's - a young Gallic woman who resisted the advances of a Roman governor justly named Olibrius and who gave her life for her Christian faith. A tragedy written in 1877 recounts the tale - the **Mystery Play** staged in Alise during the festivities held on 7th September (costumed procession).

General view of Semur.

SEMUR-EN-AUXOIS

This wonderful fortified town has often provided inspiration for film directors. Gene Kelly (*Happy Journey*), Louis de Funès (*Ni vu ni connu*), and Philippe Noiret (*Clérambard*) have all worked here. Set against the background of pastures and thickets that form the Auxois region, Semur stands proudly above a meander of the R.Armançon. Its foundations are the famous pink granite - now also the name of a local sweet.

The mediaeval town is reached by way of the Sauvigny and 14th-century Guillier Gates and the Joly Bridge (1786). Once connected by curtain walls, the towers are now isolated - Prison Tower, Margot Tower, Géhenne Tower, and the **Orle d'or** whose top was originally decorated with a circle of gilded metal. The tower is 144 ft. high and has walls that are 20 ft. thick at the base. It has a long scar dating from the siege of 1589.

The collegiate church of Notre-Dame, parts of which were built in the 13th century, was restored by Viollet-le-Duc. The church is said to

45

Semur, jutting out of the heart of the Auxois region.

Notre-Dame Church and the Pinard Bridge. ▶

have been given an astonishing relic brought back from the Holy Land in the Middle Ages - the Virgin Mary's wedding ring ! The tympanum on the **Bleds Portal** (14th century) provides a lively account of the life of St.Thomas.

The **Ring Race** has been run every year since 1639, on 31st May. It is the oldest horse race in France. The win-

ner (over 2,052 meters) receives a gold ring bearing the town's coat-of-arms. Before this, the **Hosiery Race** had been run every year since 1369 on 31st May when the prize was a pair of knitted hose. An annual road race was recreated in 1978, on the Sunday before or after 31st May.

The 80-hectare **Lac de Pont** near Semur is a dam built in 1883 to

supply water to the Burgundy canal. Beach, angling, sailing etc.

Nearby : the **Château de Bourbilly** (memorabilia relating to St.Jeanne de Chantal and Madame de Sévigné), the extraordinary **St.Thibault's Church**, and the **Thil Motte** (remains of a castle and a collegiate church).

EPOISSES (Château)

The **Château d'Epoisses** looks like an apple cut in two. Half of it disappeared during the French Revolution and the other has two faces - the rather rough "skin" on the outside, and the façade overlooking the courtyard which is a pleasantly motley construction, a happy or, in short, kindly face.

In the 6th century, Queen Brunehault, regent of the kingdom of Austrasia (stretching from Champagne to the Rhine), made frequent visits to this fortress, which was one of the most solidly-built in Burgundy. The **Condé Tower** serves as reminder that the Great Condé owned Epoisses from 1667 to 1672. The château has had many an illustrious visitor - Henri IV, **Madame de Sévigné,** Chateaubriand etc. It has now belonged to the Guitaut family for the past three hundred years. They have the only set of letters handwritten by Madame de Sévigné (76 in all).

The outer courtyard was used as a refuge for the villagers in times of war. The early 15th-century **dovecot** contains 3,000 pigeonholes, which means that the estate stretched over some 3,000 hectares in those days.

Epoisses is also famous for its cheese. Made from cow's milk, it is a soft cheese with a pinkish washed rind. The washing process using marc de bourgogne gives it a distinctive taste.

A few miles away are the **Château de Bourbilly** (memorabilia relating to St.Jeanne de Chantal and Madame de Sévigné) and the **Serein Valley.**

General view of the castle.

SAULIEU

How could you possibly stay on the motorway for lunch or dinner when you're on a level with Saulieu? Among the restaurants in this small town is the flagship of them all, Alexandre Dumaine's admirable **Côte d'Or**. One day he threw the visitors' book filled with signatures of the famous into the fire because a rather unintelligent tourist had written two lines of verse in it where Dumaine rhymed with "bedaine" (pot belly).

Bernard Loiseau has come to roost in the **Côte d'Or** and has given it back its original splendour.

Saulieu is an ancient place of pilgrimage and has always been a stop-over point. Yet Christians from the Orient, Andoche and Thyrse, were martyred here in the 2nd century. Charlemagne had a church built here, near a Benedictine abbey. Until the 13th century, the Bishops of Autun were Counts of Saulieu. **St. Andoche's Basilica** (late 11th century) has lost the chancel that was rebuilt in the 18th century. Very picturesque capitals. **Treasure** (the so-called "Charlemagne Gospels" dating from the 12th century, with binding of ivory plates carved in Italy in the 6th century - a copy is on show in the basilica).

Saulieu was the home of the Burgundian historian Claude Courtépée (1721-1781) and of the animal sculptor François Pompon (1855-1933) who suddenly rose to fame at the age of 68 for his Polar Bear exhibited at the Salon d'Automne (there is a copy of it in the Darcy Gardens in Dijon). Alongside the R.N.6 road is Pompon's statue of a Bull, erected in 1948. The model for the sculpture belonged to Edouard Herriot.

Two capitals representing the flight into Egypt (top) and the hanging of Judas (bottom).

50

Scenery in the Morvan.

Overleaf: The famous tympanum in Autun cathedral.

THE MORVAN REGIONAL PARK

The Morvan Regional Park, which extends over nearly 200,000 hectares and some 70 villages and towns, lies on a granite upland full of forests and streams. The **Maison du Parc** (Park Centre) is in **Saint-Brisson** near Montsauche. Among its outstanding beauty spots is **Mont-Beuvray** (2,672 ft.), a focal point in Ancient Gaul (Bibracte, the capital of the Eduen tribe, where Vercingétorix was appointed chief of the army that was to confront Caesar). The Beuvray

Festivities are held early in July, and the Chestnut Fair in Saint-Léger at the end of October. The spa of **Saint-Honoré-les-Bains** caters for those suffering from asthma, lung problems, and bronchial disorders. Louis Malle shot his film *Murmur of the Heart* there. The village of **Anost** is particularly attractive.

Many manmade lakes : **Lac des Settons** built in 1858 (359 hectares) in Moux and Montsauche, the **Pannesière Dam** (1949, 520 hectares) in

Chaumard, **Lac de Chaumeçon** (1935, 135 hectares) near Lormes, **Lac de Saint-Aignan** (1968, 142 hectares) in Saint-Aignan, and **Lac du Crescent** (1933, 165 hectares) near Marigny-l'Eglise etc.

In **Château-Chinon,** the astonishing **Septennate Museum** created by François Mitterand is worth a visit.

Abbaye de la Pierre-qui-Vire in Saint-Léger-Vauban, founded in 1850.

51

The St. Andrew Gate.

Close-up of the Nativity capital on which Joseph ▶
is depicted showing enormous sympathy.

AUTUN

Autun was born on **Mont-Beuvray,** or Bibracte, the capital of the Eduens. Gaul's organisational policy as decided by Caesar Augustus led to the founding of a new town on a site that was easier to reach - Augustodunum, traditionally said to have been founded in 15 B.C. Autun celebrated its two thousandth anniversary in 1985.

Throughout the days of the Gallo-Roman civilisation, Autun was an intellectual, artistic, religious and economic centre. The town still has a number of reminders of its glorious origins (Autun considers itself to be "the sister and rival of Rome" or "the Gallic Rome") - the **amphitheatre** which could cater for 15,000 spectators, the **Temple of Janus** (a borrowed name) etc. Aerial photographs have recently revealed the existence of other buildings (in particular a second amphitheatre outside the walls). **St.Andrew's Gate** (1st century, rebuilt by Viollet-le-Duc). **Arroux Gate** (same period).

Of the 4th and 11th centuries, the town has little to show. Although often ravaged by invasion, Autun still has some large monasteries. The builder bishop Etienne de Bagé had **St.Lazarus'** built in the 12th century with the assistance of an artistic genius from Rome, the sculptor **Gislebertus.** When the belltower collapsed in the 15th century, Cardinal Rolin had to have the steeple and the upper section of the chancel rebuilt. Viollet-le-Duc was involved in the 19th-century restoration work carried out on the cathedral (the spire and pillars were rebuilt).

Gislebertus' **tympanum** had been plastered over in 1766 because the canons considered it to be a barbaric piece of work ! In doing so, the head was broken off the statue of Christ, a gesture wrongfully attributed to Voltaire. Canon Denis Grivot (a love of Autun made flesh) found the head and put it back in its rightful place in 1948. Gislebertus is one

Panoramic view of Autun.

of the few mediaeval sculptors known by his name - he signed his work (beneath Christ's feet on the tympanum). He may have worked in Cluny, and he almost certainly passed through Vézelay. He is thought to have created the carvings in Autun between 1125 and 1145. But although Autun's 12th-century school of sculpture has left some of its work in place, the same cannot be said of the manuscripts written in Autun in the Early Middle Ages - they are now in libraries in Munich and the Vatican.

Charles-Maurice de Talleyrand-Périgord spent only one month in his archbishopric, from 12th March to 12th April 1789, just long enough to campaign for, and have himself elected to, the States General.

The **Rolin Museum** houses the items found during digs on Bibracte, along with a variety of works and a few masterpieces e.g. Gislebertus' Sleeping Eve which comes from the cathedral (the most extraordinary picture of a woman ever inspired by the Middle Ages), the Nativity by the Maître de Moulins (c.1480), the Autun Madonna (15th century) in painted stone etc. (Museum closed Tuesdays). The town also has an Archaeological Museum and a Natural History Museum.

The **Promenade des Marbres** in the shade of the limetrees leads to the **Military Academy** beyond a formal garden laid out by Le Nôtre. This was originally a Sulpicius seminary (18th century). The Bonaparte brothers and Lazare Carnot were pupils in a Jesuit college here, now the Bonaparte High School.

Autun is also well-known to geologists. In 1881, the sedimentation in this basin led to the creation of the term "Autunian" (the Lower Permian Period). The **bituminous shale** used by the Romans was exploited industrially from 1824 onwards to produce shale oil by a process of distillation. It was used to enrich water-based gas for Dijon's lighting system. Production ceased in 1957. The conical tips at **Les Télots** bear witness to the importance of this industry some one hundred years ago.

Two capitals in the chapter house : the flight into Egypt (top) and the hanging of Judas (bottom).

SULLY (Château)

"This is the Versailles of Burgundy", said Madame de Sévigné, writing of the **Château de Sully.**

Situated at the head of the valley of the R.Drée whose waters flow into the castle moat, Sully bears the name of a family which died out in the 13th century. The old château belonged to the Couches, Montaigus, Rabutins and de Saulx-Tavannes. Gaspart de Saulx-Tavannes (1509-1573), Maréchal of France, Lieutenant General of Burgundy and, later, governor of Provence, began the reconstruction of Sully. The task was continued by his widow with the help of the architect Nicolas Ribonnier and, later, of his son Jean, a former Leaguer who had rallied Henri IV's camp. Some of the mediaeval features have been retained.

The vast quadrilateral preceded by a long courtyard flanked by box hedges is without doubt one of the most majestic aristocratic residences in Burgundy. The building dates from the 16th and 17th centuries. The wall and terraces overlooking the lake were commissioned by the Morey family (18th century). Sully passed into the hands of the Mac-Mahons in the mid 18th century, and they have remained the owners up to the present day. It was here that Edme-Patrice de Mac-Mahon was born in 1808. He was to become Duc de Magenta, Maréchal of France, and the first President of the Third Republic which he remained until 1879. He is wrongfully remembered for nothing more than a few legendary sayings that have all been held up to ridicule e.g. "What a lot of water!" when faced with floods.

The chapel, rebuilt in the Gothic style c.1830, was again altered in the latter years of the 19th century. The cannon balls and stone pyramids decorating the stone bridge across the moat also date from this period. A theatre was set out in one section of the outhouses in 1840.

The Château de Sully.

58

CHATEAUNEUF EN-AUXOIS

Châteauneuf, an old Auxois village perched on a hilltop like a crow's nest, overlooks the entire Vandenesse Valley, the Burgundy Canal, the Paris-Lyons motorway, and the railway line. Back in the 12th century, Jean de Châteauneuf had a well-fortified house on the site. The estate was confiscated by Philip the Good, Duke of Burgundy, and given to Philippe Pot.

The **castle** is a fine building with its square 12th-century keep and its 13th-century walls. The main building dates from the days of Philippe Pot (15th century) whose motto can be seen on one of the chimneys "Tant L.Vault". The Flamboyant Gothic architecture is reminiscent of the Duke's Residence in Dijon.

Many items from Dijon's museum and public library were stored in the castle during the Second World War, as were the Côte-d'Or's public records.

COMMARIN (Château)

The Château de Commarin, standing amidst fine outhouses, a vast moat, and a large English-style park, was built mainly between 1620 and 1711. But there had been a fortified mansion on the site since the 12th century, and a fortress replaced it in the 15th century (the circular towers are still standing). The Vienne family owned Commarin from 1500 to 1744.

The Vogüé family have been the owners since the early years of last century and Count and Countess Louis de Vogüé are only too pleased to open the house to visitors (Easter to All Saints' Day excl. Tues. - on the Dukes of Burgundy Route).

Behind the Classical façades is the home of a great lady of the 18th century, Marie-Judith de Vienne, Marquise d'Antigny - and the house has been kept intact by her descendents. Among the most interesting works of art in the château are four 16th-century armorial tapestries made on the occasion of the Dinteville-Pontailler and Dinteville-Vienne marriages, and the triptych given by Girard de Vienne to the Sainte-Chapelle in Dijon.

Although he was born and died in Dijon, the writer Henri Vincenot (1912-1985) lived in Commarin for many years, in a small house near the château. It was here that he wrote *La Billebaude, Le Pape des Escargots,* etc.

Panoramic view of Dijon. In the foreground, the Flora Courtyard in the Palace of the States of Burgundy.

The Bar Tower. ▶

Overleaf : Palace of the State of Burgundy

DIJON

Kingdom, duchy, province... today, Dijon is the capital of the Burgundy region. Lying in the heart of an urban district with a population of 230,000, the town always enchants visitors. It escaped damage during the wars and has 100 hectares of the most beautiful old town centre in the whole country. Its parks and gardens once won it the title of "top ecological town in France". It is a pleasure to eat out there, there are numerous museums, and the pedestrian precincts in the old town have a delightful charm all of their own.

Dijon has never had a cult figure, never had one single monument towering massively above the others. In short, there is a pervading sense of balance and harmony. The Rue de la Liberté remains the main street in a town that has taken care to keep enough time to enjoy life.

The town hall is housed in the **Palace of the Dukes and States of Burgundy,** built over a period of five hundred years on the site of the long-gone former residence of the Capetian dukes. The **Bar Tower** on the Cour de Bar was built in 1365, commissioned by Philip the Bold. King René of Anjou, Duc de Bar, was imprisoned there. The **Ducal Kitchens** date from 1433, when Philip the Good occupied the throne. A

whole ox could be roasted in each of the six monumental fireplaces. The chamber is now used by the town council when receiving special guests.

In 1450-1455, Philip the Good commissioned Jean Poncelet to build the main section of the Ducal Palace (ground floor rooms of the town hall, guardroom in the Art Gallery). The **Philip the Good Tower** (or the Terrace Tower - but the locals insist on calling it the Bar Tower) dates from this same period. It towers 169 ft. above the Palace of the States of Burgundy, giving the palace a scale and a touch of fantasy. The States were the assembly attended by the three orders of Burgundy (nobility,

The Chamber of the States of Burgundy.

The staircase designed by Jacques Gabriel. ▶

clergy, and Third Estate) which convened from time to time in Dijon. It was for this assembly that, in the late 17th century, Jules Hardouin-Mansart designed the first wing of a new palace and the fine Place Royale (or Place de la Libération) which was built to take the equestrian statue of Louis XIV that was melted down during the French Revolution. Most of the buildings date from the 18th century.

The **Jacques Gabriel staircase** was built in 1735 and is one of the finest in France because of its majestic elegance. It leads up to the **State Assembly Room,** once the meeting chamber of the provincial assembly. The interior decoration was badly damaged during the Revolution but was replaced in 1895 by the official Third Republic Style. The painting of the Glories of Burgundy, by Henry-Léopold Lévy, is impressive - at least for its gilt frame.

The recently-restored Cour de Flore contains the **Chapel of the Chosen Few** (Chapelle des Elus), designed by Pierre le Mousseux in the Versailles style (1739). Wood panelling by Verbeckt.

The former **Burgundy Assizes** are just a few yards away. They are now used as the town's Law Courts. Houses and mansions illustrate all the developments in vernacular architecture from the 15th to the 18th centuries - there are some fifty remarkable buildings.

The largest parish in the town is **Notre-Dame** and the church dates from 1210-1240. Its West Front is decorated with gargoyles which were recarved in the 19th century and is unique in France. The tympana above the doorways were damaged during the Revolution. The height of the very narrow nave gives added brilliance to the stained glass windows, especially the rose window in the north arm of the transept (13th century). The lantern tower and spire are an unfortunate piece of 19th-century restoration.

St.Bénigne's used to be the minster of a Benedictine abbey situated beyond the castrum. The monastery had been founded in the 6th century when the Bishop of Langres autho-

Opposite, top : The Place Royale, now the Place de la Libération.

Opposite, bottom : The Romanesque crypt in St.Bénigne's Church.

rised worship on the tomb of St.Bénigne, an apostle and martyr of Dijon whose existence now appears to be far from certain. There was a Merovingian basilica on the site, then a Carolingian basilica which was replaced between 1001 and 1020 by a church commissioned by Guillaume de Volpiano, Abbot of St.Bénigne and a Benedictine renovator.

The great Romanesque church used to be a circular three-storey building set beyond a chancel and standing over St.Bénigne's crypt. The rotunda was demolished during the French Revolution. The crypt was rediscovered in the mid 19th century and is now open to the public. As for the main building, it underwent complete reconstruction in the Gothic style between 1280 and the early 14th century. St. Bénigne's became a cathedral at the time of the Revolution. The damaged mediaeval tympanum was replaced during the Empire by the tympanum from the former cathedral, St.Stephen's. This explains why it shows the martyrdom of St. Stephen, sculpted by J.-B. and E. Bouchardon (1720). In 1894, a new spire was built above the transept crossing ; it is said to be the tallest and most slender steeple in France. There is a very attractive chime on the quarter hour.

St. Michael's Church, which is astonishing for its Renaissance West Front, in fact dates from the transitional period. The building itself is Flamboyant Gothic (late 15th century) and when the idea of a West Front was mooted (early 16th century), tastes had changed. Then the Renaissance style gradually gave way to Classicisim. The lantern turrets date from 1667.

Clairvaux Abbey has left us the two-storey **Clairvaux Cellars.**

The central library is housed in the former **Jesuit College Chapel** built c.1610. An exceedingly fine reading room...

Bossuet, Rameau, President de Brosses, Piron, Crébillon, Cazotte, Rude, Cabet, Estaunié, and Eiffel were all born in Dijon, as was the author Henri Vincenot, the former Minister of Culture Jean-Philippe Lecat, the actor Claude Jade and the winner of the Nobel Prize for Medecine Roger Guillemin (who now has American citizenship). But the birthplace is of little importance... The

Academy of Dijon was the first one to honour Jean-Jacques Rousseau, in 1750.

Popular and legendary characters abound. First of all, there is the stone owl left on one of the flying buttresses of Notre-Dame. As people pass it, in the Rue de la Chouette, they stroke it and make a wish. In the church, Notre-Dame du Bon Espoir (Our Lady of Hope), there is a falsely-named Black Virgin which is, in fact, the oldest wooden statue of

St.Michael's Church.

the Virgin Mary anywhere in France (11th century). "An unprecedented piece of work", according to Malraux. It has been worshipped for nine centuries and is still the town's patron. On the West Front are the gargoyles that were originally removed because of the potential danger if they fell. They were later recarved and put back in place c.1880. And up above Notre-Dame are Jacquemart and his family. Philip the Bold confiscated the clock from Courtrai in 1382. Jacquemart is an archetypal local, ringing out the hours and drawing on his pipe, and he has had a wife, Jacqueline, since the 17th century. Jacquelinet was born in 1716 and Jacquelinette in 1881. The 20th century has not yet given them another child...

The Bear, by Pompon.

The "Bareuzai", on the Place François-Rude.

The Chamber of Tombs in the Art Gallery.

On the Place François-Rude is the "Bareuzai", a statue representing a Dijon winegrower crushing grapes in a vat (sculpture by Jules Gérard). On the Place Darcy is a replica of the polar bear statue that "launched" François Pompon. In the new Petit-Cîteaux district, there is a carving of a young girl's head which seems to be emerging from the ground on one of the squares - it is a recent work by Denis Mondineu.

The **Art Gallery** is housed in part of the former Palace of the Dukes and States of Burgundy. It stands on the site of the Sainte-Chapelle that was unfortunately demolished in the early years of the 19th century. The guardroom was refurbished in 1827 in a Romantic style ready for the tombs of Philip the Bold and John the Fearless that were originally in Champmol. The reredos by Jacques de Baërze also came from the Car-

thusian monastery that was razed to the ground. The **Nativity** is by Maître de Flémalle. The mourners on the Dukes' tombs are a marvel of mediaeval statuary (by Claus Sluter and his followers).

In addition to large collections of old paintings (primitives, Italian art etc.), the gallery has, for the past few years, housed the extraordinary **Granville Donation** of modern and contemporary art, which was given to the town by Pierre and Kathleen Granville. In particular, it has the largest public collection of works by Nicolas de Staël, Vieira da Silva etc. The **Magnin Museum** in the Rue des Bons-Enfants has retained the atmosphere of the personal collection of two enlightened amateurs called Jeanne and Maurice Magnin who died shortly before the last war. An astonishing "home" museum !

In the former Benedictine abbey of Saint-Bénigne, the **Archaeology Museum** recounts the entire history of Man in Burgundy. There are numerous items relating to the Gauls (Sources of the R.Seine).

The **Arquebuse Botanical Gardens** (once the shooting range used by the arquebusiers of Dijon) contain some 3,500 species of plant. Their seed catalogue is sent out every year to 560 botanical gardens and institutes all over the world. Medicinal herb garden (192 different species). Arboretum and Temple of Love, glasshouses, temporary exhibitions.

Dijon's gastronomy comes to the fore during the international trade and food fair (end October-early November), and during the States General of French food and high-quality fare etc. The "town with the 100 belltowers" that so astonished François I has become the town with the 100 chefs' hats. Cooking has its set programme here - eggs poached in wine, snails, jellied ham with parsley, coq au vin, chicken à la Gaston-Gérard (former Mayor of Dijon who founded the fair), hare à la Piron, and blackcurrant desserts.

Dijon mustard was mentioned in texts as far back as the 14th century. Everybody but everybody made it. In 1636, the profession of vinegar- and mustard-maker became more organised. In the 19th century, the Dijon Academy looked at the problem and tried to draw up criteria of quality. The so-called Dijon mustard is produced by sieving the seeds of black or brown mustard, crushing them, and emulsifying them without herbs or spices in verjuice (a very immature wine obtained by pressing unripe grapes, or simply a bitter wine). The name is not protected by a patent and is used throughout the world. But it always applies to a strong spicy mustard. Mustard pots have become collectors' items (Museum of Burgundian Life).

IN THE VICINITY :

• To the south towards Beaune is the **canal port.** The obelisk (or, rather, the pyramid) dates from 1786 and commemmorates the joining of three seas by means of Burgundy's canal network. The first stone of the Burgundy canal (linking the rivers Yonne and Saône) was laid in 1784 by the Prince de Condé at the Saint-Jean-de-Losne Lock. Monument to **Gustave Eiffel** sculpted by Robert Rigot.

To the west toward Pouilly-en-Auxois, is the former **Carthusian monastery of Champmol.** Philip the Bold brought 24 Carthusian monks to Dijon with their prior, and had a great monastery built for them by Flemish craftsmen and artists, with a church designed to become the ''St.Denis of the Dukes of Burgundy''. Claus Sluter and his nephew, Claus de Werve, worked here, as did other image-makers, providing the decorative features for the church and the tombs of Philip the Bold and Jean the Fearless. Other remains of this work include the portal and the magnificent ''Well of Moses'' designed as the centre-piece of the large cloister. Claus Sluter's six prophets are among the finest pieces of sculpture of their day - his figure of Moses is the only one that bears comparison with the one carved by Michaelangelo. The Carthusian monastery was demolished after the Revolution by one Emmanuel Crétet, Napoleon's Minister of the Interior and... the so-called Comte de Champmol !

To the north-west towards Châtillon-sur-Seine is **Talant.** From the platform where the **castle** of the Dukes of Burgundy once stood (it was demolished in 1598), there is a fine view of Dijon. All that remains of the castle are the recently-restored cellars with their ogival vaulting. Talant **church,** which dates partly from the 13th century, houses a large number of works of art.

Large private house with Burgundy-style roof.

Château and vineyard of Gevrey-Chambertin.

COTE DE NUITS

"The Champs Elysées of Burgundy" - the famous Côte d'Or from Dijon to Meursault. The Cote de Nuits (most of the great red wines made from the Pinot Noir grape) begins in Marsannay and runs as far as Corgoloin. Follow the **Route des Grands Crus** from Dijon to Vougeot.

In Fixin, there is the Perrière Manor that was once used by the monks of Cîteaux as a convalescent home. 14th-century church and fine lavabo (1827). Attractive Romanesque church in Fixey. Sculpture by Fransois Rude (**Napoleon's awakening**) commissioned by Claude Noisot, a veteran of the Napoleonic Wars (1847). Small Napoleonic museum.

Clos de la Perrière, du Chapitre and Napoléon.

Now a secondary school, the **Château de Brochon** was built in 1900 to resemble Azay-le-Rideau. It was commissioned by Stéphen Liégard who invented the expression "Côte d'Azur".

The upper town of **Gevrey-Chambertin** has a 15th- and 16th-century castle and a 12th- and 13th-century church. Between Gevrey and Morey, you will find the **Chambertin** and **Chambertin Clos de Bèze** vineyards as well as the outer ring - **Mazis, Charmes, Ruchottes,** etc.

Morey-Saint-Denis : Clos de la Roche, Clos de Tart, Clos Saint-Denis, Bonnes-Mares (also in Chambolle), **Clos des Lambrays. Chambolle-Musigny :** the famous **Musigny. Vougeot :** see the chapter on the Clos de Vougeot.

Vosné-Romanée is a land of pure delight : **Romanée, Romanée-Conti, Romanée-Saint-Vivant, La Tâche, Richebourg, La Grande Rue.** The **Echézeaux** and the **Grands-Echézeaux** are to be found in Flagey-Echézeaux

Beyond Nuits-Saint-Georges is the **Comblanchien Quarry** which provided the stone for the Paris Opera House, the steps of the Sacré-Cœur, Orly Airport, and the base of the Statue of Liberty in New York (it is a very hard limestone).

CLOS DE VOUGEOT
(Château)

The Clos de Vougeot is the Acropolis of Burgundy, but it is first and foremost 50 hectares and 85 ares of walled vineyard, producing one of the best red wines in the world. "All the aroma of springtime". A well-rounded wine... a really straightforward wine that expresses all the genius of the Pinot Noir grape.

It is also a fine winegrower's château, well anchored in the earth, an elegant functional building. In short, "a corner of paradise on earth," as Gaston Roupnel wrote.

Created on 16th November 1934 in Nuits-Saint-Georges, the **Brotherhood of the Knights of Winetasting** (Confrérie des Chevaliers du Taste-vin, whose motto is "Never in vain, always in wine") bought the château in November 1944. It holds its assemblies there, and some twenty times a year welcomes more than 500 guests from every corner of the globe. The Clos de Vougeot, the head of a Brotherhood that has a membership of 10,000 spread over all five continents, has become the temple of the Burgundian soul. The Brotherhood has a wide range of activities (St. Vincent Procession on the last Saturday in January, Taste-vinage, The Three Glories on the 3rd weekend in November etc.). It owns no vines itself and sells no wine.

As for the vines at Le Clos, they remained the property of a single grower until 1889. Today, there are 80 owners (with plots of land of 5.48 hectares down to 8.86 ares) sharing the prestigious estate which produces an average of 200,000 bottles every year.

The Clos de Vougeot was created by Cîteaux, which is almost ten miles away, and it gradually gained in importance over the centuries. The first donations (1110) were contemporary with the founding of the abbey. The present, intangible limits of the Clos were fixed between the 12th and 15th centuries. The **Romanesque cellar** (88 ft. long and 57 ft. high) on ground level was built in the 13th century. It has no vaulting. The **manorhouse** was built by the 48th Abbot of Cîteaux, Jean Loisier, in 1551.

The estate was declared national property during the French Revolution and passed through several hands before being purchased by the Ouvrard family in 1818. The château was restored with the assistance of an architect called Félix Vionnois in 1891. At that time, the owner was a wine merchant named Léonce Bocquet, a picturesque character who had a red carpet almost 2 miles long laid from the château to the church in Gilly for his daughter's wedding. When he died in 1913, Léonce Bocquet was buried in front of the château, as he had requested.

The Clos du Vougeot château is open throughout the year (except between Christmas and New Year). Visitors see a château that is built on a human scale, a château wise enough not to submerge the vineyard in a misplaced sense of vanity. The Renaissance style is more orderly here, corrected by Burgundians with heads firmly on their shoulders. The **fermenting chamber** described by Rabelais for its "Gargantuan" character, has all the intimacy of a clois-

ter. The four huge presses with oak capstans date from the same period as the foundation of the Clos. They stand at regular intervals in galleries that are 97 ft. long and 32 ft. wide. In the centre is the "Basket Carrier" (a wine-grower carrying his basket on his shoulder at harvest time) by Henri Bouchard (1960).

Old wine press in Le Clos de Vougeot.

The Romanesque cellar.

NUITS-SAINT-GEORGES

"Old customs and flourishing businesses" -this was how Gaston Roupnel described Nuits-Saint-Georges. It lies in the heart of the Côte, and is the choicest morsel of wine-growing Burgundy. Its 17th century belfry towers over the hustle and bustle of firms specialising in the wine trade, many of them founded early in the 19th century, and over busy manufacturing companies (making liqueurs, fruit juice, etc.)

The **Les Bolards Gallo-Roman site** provided experts with some very interesting finds. The town's history is linked to the nearby Abbey of Cîteaux and the powerful House of Vergy in the Hautes-Côtes. **St.Symphorian's** (13th century) is one of the most beautiful churches in the Côte.

In 1693, Fagon prescribed a daily, but moderate, intake of "old Burgundy" for Louis XIV. The advice given by the physician to the Sun-King became famous, and probably applied to Nuits-Saint-Georges which thereafte enjoyed an excellent reputation. "The stomach retains and digests the Burgundy without attempting to rid itself of it", he wrote.

The Saint-Georges are the foremost of all the premiers crus produced in the parish. The Brotherhood of the Knights of Winetasting was founded in Nuits-Saint-Georges on 16th November 1934, and in doing so Camille Rodier and Georges Faiveley invented - a public relations exercise.

The museum (11 Rue Camille-Rodier) is open. The exhibits include Gallo-Roman furniture from the digs at Les Bolards, tombstones from the graveyard, and some of the Merovingian furniture from the necropolis of Argilly, etc.

The Belfry in Nuits-Saint-Georges (photo by H. Champollion).

The Vergy plateau.

VERGY

The "area up the hill" forms a plateau between the Côte and the Ouche Valley. To the north are the Hautes-Côtes de Nuits; to the south the Côtes de Beaune. Traditional fruit-farming (blackcurrants, raspberries, redcurrants, and strawberries).

Around the year 1000 A.D., the powerful influence of Vergy spread throughout the immediate vicinity, over Burgundy as a whole, and well beyond its frontiers.

Vergy is the mystic hillside of the Hautes-Côtes. Its outline, like a ship wrecked on a shore, serves as a reminder of its long voyage through History. The Ancient Burgundians and Francs both settled there.

On the hill at Vergy (signposted footpaths, orientation tables) is the former **Saint-Vivant Monastery.** It is first mentioned towards the end of the 9th century.

The monastery, standing on the south side of Vergy Hill, became a daughter house of the famous Abbey of Cluny in 1095. It then held the rank of "grand priory of Cluny".

There were a number of large buildings on the site but they all lay in ruins when, in the mid 18th century, the nine monks of Saint-Vivant decided to modernise their monastery. Grandiose projects were discussed. Only one, a more modest affair, was completed between 1772 and 1787, on the site of the abbey that had been razed to the ground. It was a sort of small one-storey castle. Part of the church is still standing. Visitors can now see the two-storey cellar that was once underneath the monks' cells.

The rebuilding had only just been completed when the community was abolished, in 1788. A few monks continued to live there until 1790.

The plain, rustic, well-designed **Museum of Hautes-Côtes Arts and Traditions,** opened in 1974 in Reulle-Vergy by the Association of the Friends of Vergy with the help of the town council, houses an exhibition showing various aspects of the Hautes-Côtes (geology, physical geography, history of its settlements through the ages, flora and fauna etc.) and Vergy (history, literary and musical traditions etc.).

In the vicinty (Hautes Côtes-de-Nuits) are the **Château d'Entre-Deux-Monts** built c. 1656

The Château d'Entre-Deux-Monts.

(Concoeur-et-Corboin), the **Château de Collonges-les-Bévy** (17th century), and the **Maison des Hautes-Côtes** in Marey-les-Fussey.

The poet Alphonse de Lamartine was a frequent visitor to the **Château de Montculot** (Urcy) between 1801 when he was aged 11 and 1831. In 1826, on his uncle's death, he became the owner of the château, which he sold in 1831 with the 365 hectares of land and woods. It was here that he came after the death of Elvira and that he wrote *La Source dans les Bois*.

CITEAUX (Abbey)

St.Bernard wanted a building devoid of all ornamentation - in Cîteaux, the buildings have little charm and the decoration is no more than plain. Some fifty monks pray and work here, as they did almost 900 years ago. The monastic day begins at 3.15 a.m. in the winter and 3.45 a.m. in the summer. It ends at 8 p.m. in winter and 8.30 p.m. in summer. Mass is said on Sundays at 10.45 a.m.

The Abbey of Notre-Dame de Cîteaux was founded in 1098 by St.Robert de Molesme on a plain covered with reeds (or "cistels", hence the abbey's name). The "New Monastery" sought the life of poverty and austerity experienced by the monks of earlier years, based on the Rule of St.Benedict. In 1112, Bernard de Fontaine (the future St.Bernard) came to the community with some twenty young noblemen from the vicinity. This was a decisive moment in the abbey's development. It shook the Christian world of the 12th century and within 40 years the humble abbey at Cîteaux had become the head of an order of 343 abbeys, all of them daughter-houses or daughters of daughter-houses. The third foundation, Clairvaux, had Bernard as its first Abbot. Stephen Harding, Abbot of Cîteaux from 1108 to 1133, was also canonised.

There have been up to 500 monks in Cîteaux. The abbey played a major role in the development of Burgundy's wine industry, especially at the **Clos de Vougeot.** It was abolished during the French Revolution, emptied of its treasures, and later turned into a country house, a refinery, a phalanstery under the sociologist Young, then a "disciplinary colony", a centre for young delinquents opened by Father Rey who commissioned the church we see today (dating from 1868). In 1892, the Cistercian monks became members of the Cistercian Order of Strict Observance. In 1898, thanks to a donation, they again came to Cîteaux. Now the mother-house of 120 monasteries and convents throughout the world, Cîteaux remains the spiritual heart of the Order. Yet the Abbot General lives in Rome. The present abbey exploits a 240-hectare farm. It no longer owns any vineyards but it produces a highly-esteemed cheese called **cîteaux.**

From the Seurre road, you can see the former library (15th century). The monks live in a building erected in the late 18th century by Nicolas Lenoir "the Roman"; it was the wing of a larger building which was never completed.

The abbey is not open to the public but there is an audiovisual exhibition at the gatehouse. It is, though, possible to come here for a retreat or as a paying guest (hotel facilities).

Burgundy countryside.

79

The hospital in Beaune : the great "Paupers' Room".

The magnificent roof of the Hospice. ▶

BEAUNE

"I should like to be drowned in a vat of Beaune wine so that my death is effortless and good", the Duke of Clarence is recorded to have said when condemned to be beheaded by his brother, the King of England. You don't have to go that far.. but in Beaune it is difficult to avoid the subject of wine. Outside the town, the vineyards cover 580 hectares, most of them producing reds. The premiers crus are produced on 320 hectares - Bressandes, Clos des Mouches (here meaning "wasps" rather than "flies"), Marconnets, Grèves etc. The **Côte de Beaune** stretches from Aloxe-Corton to Chagny (3,000 hectares).

The capital of Burgundy wines : with a trade that was already flourishing in the Middle Ages and links throughout the Christian world, the **Wine Trading Houses** were establis-hed in Beaune in the 18th century. Life inside these companies is like a pitch black night. A trip **down to the cellars** is one of the vital ceremonials of any visit to Beaune - and the choice of cellar is far from limited.

The town's coat-of-arms includes a Madonna and Child, and the Child Jesus is shown holding a bunch of grapes in His hand, of course. By praying to this miraculous statue, the Carmelite nun Marguerite Parigot obtained from Heaven the joyous conception of Louis XIV who was born to Anne of Austria after 23 years of sterility. The Carmelites used to own the Child Jesus Vineyard (3.9 hectares in the Grèves), producing one of the region's best wines.

In the Hôtel-Dieu (hospital), note the "Paupers' Ward", the chapel, the dispensary, and of course the museum.

The wonderful **Last Judgement Reredos** by Roger Van der Weyden (known in Belgium as Rogier de La Pasture !) is one of the 17th-century masterpieces that belonged to the Dukes of Burgundy. Founded in 1443 by Nicolas Rolin, Chancellor to the Duke of Burgundy, the hospital was built to designs used for the Saint-Jean Hospice in Valenciennes and drawn by a Flemish architect. The first nuns cames from Malines. Despite the Belgian connection, the roof of varnished tiles has become a symbol of Burgundy for the tourists - Beaune stands at a major motorway junction and has always been a melting-pot of various cultures and civilisations.

The Hospices de Beaune came into being in 1805, when the Hôtel-Dieu and the Hospice de la Charité were combined. They own the largest estate in the region - 538 hectares of

woodland, 10 farms and 773 hectares of meadows and fields, in addition to 53 hectares of vines producing very high-class wines. Twentyone people are employed by the Hospices to look after the prestigious vineyard - and locally this is regarded as conferring almost aristocratic status. The vineyards lie in the Côte de Beaune and in Gevrey-Chambertin (Mazis-Chambertin) and Morey Saint-Denis (Clos de la Roche). Since 1859, the **auction of the Hospices' wines** draws huge crowds on the third Sunday in November - the second day of the "Three Glories" (Winetasters' chapter on the previous days, and Paulée de Meursault on the next). The auction continues for as long as the auctioneer's candle burns and the bids soar as one candle is replaced by another.

In summer, Beaune is like Lourdes. Leave the crowds of the Hôtel-Dieu behind you and take a look at the **Notre-Dame basilica,** "a Romanesque building wearing a Gothic overmantle" (13th century) where the Flemish tapestries illustrate the life of the Virgin Mary (1500). The **Burgundy Wine Museum** is housed in the former palace of the Dukes of Burgundy (14th - 17th centuries, modern tapestries by Jean Lurçat and Michel Tourlière). This was the first museum of local tradition to be opened in France, shortly after the war when it was created by Georges-Henri Rivière. In the town hall, a former 17th-century convent, is the **Art Gallery** (local history and works by Félix Ziem) and the **Etienne-Jules Marey Museum** with exhibits relating to the invention of chronophotography (a photograph breaking down movement into its constituent parts) which was the origin of the cinema.

The **Archéodrome** alongside the motorway brings back to life all the outstanding features of Burgundy's archaeology. The life-sized model of the fortifications of Alésia might well convince tourists in a hurry that Vercingétorix surrendered his arms to Julius Caesar on a service area of the A6...

Close-up of the polyptic by Van der Weyden (photo by H. Champollion).

A superb wine cellar in the Château de Meursault.

COTE DE BEAUNE

Whether you're on your way to, or coming from the Côte de Nuits...

From **Ladoix-Serrigny** to **Les Maranges** in Saône-et-Loire, the **Côte de Beaune** produces great red wines and the wonderful white burgundies. The Côte curves round here and the scenery becomes less rugged.

Aloxe-Corton : the **Corton-Charlemagne** (white), and the **Corton** (red and white).

Pernand-Vergelesses keeps alive the memory of Jacques Copeau (the Vieux-Colombier in Paris) who lived there from 1925 to his death in 1949.

The Château of **Savigny-les-Beaune** (18th century) was built for the Bouhier family from Dijon. Open to the public. It was in Savigny that Georges Pompidou inaugurated the Paris-Lyons motorway in 1970.

Pommard : a fine **château** dating from the days of the Directoire built by N.-J. Marey. Monopoly of the 20-hectare vineyard. Excellent red wines (cf. **Volnay**).

Meursault is a paradise of great white wines, with **Puligny-Mon-**trachet and **Chassagne-Montrachet.** The **château** in Meursault dates from the 17th century (wonderful cellars, open to the public). The premiers crus from Meursault are Perrières, Genevrières, Goutte-d'Or etc. The **Montrachet** should be "drunk on your knees with your hat off" (A. Dumas). From nearby come **Bâtard-Montrachet, Chevalier-Montrachet,** and the **Criots** and **Bienvenues-Bâtard-Montrachet.**

Santenay combines all the charms of a spa (casino) with those of a good vineyard.

LA ROCHEPOT (Château)

Left unattended and in ruins, La Rochepot became the property of the widow of President Sadi Carnot in 1893 (the family originally came from Nolay, close by). Her son had it rebuilt by Charles Suisse while Xavier Schanoski was responsible for the sculptures. The project was completed in 1926. It still belongs to the Carnot family.

La Rochepot juts out of the trees on a rocky promontory and its varnished tiles catch the light. The old castle is believed to have dated from the 12th century. As Chamberlain to Philip the Bold and a Knight of the Golden Fleece, Régnier Pot purchased it in 1403. He added a large tower, and had a 225 ft. well sunk. His son, Jacques, and his grandson, Philippe Pot, who was a confident of Charles the Bold, made a few alter-ations. The castle then passed through the hands of a number of owners, including the Cardinal de Retz. During the Revolution, it became a quarry. Luckily, La Rochepot was to be born again a century later.

Open to the public from Palm Sunday to All Saints' Day, except Tuesdays.

CHALON-SUR-SAONE

As you drive along the motorway, all you see of Chalon-sur-Sâone are the chimneys of the Saint-Gobain glassworks - the bottles used for Burgundy wines come from here. From the main road running through the town, the view is scarcely more flattering. Yet Chalon-sur-Sâone has many attractive features - romantic quays, sleepy urban districts, and old houses.

The origins of Chalon's **Carnival** have been lost in the mists of time. These days, it is synonymous with one week of exuberant festivities with a procession, decorated floats, "large-headed" characters etc.

Since 1972, the **Nicéphore-Nièpce Museum,** which is named after the inventor of photography who was born in Chalon in 1765, (the museum is housed in the former Royal Staging Post) has had numerous collections of cameras and photographic material. Nicéphore-Nièpce succeeded in creating the first-ever pictorial reproduction produced in a dark room near Chalon in 1816, using paper sensitivized with chloride and silver nitrate.

The **Denon Museum,** opened in 1819, acts as a memorial to one of Napoleon's erstwhile companions,

Vivant Denon. He was involved in the birth of Egyptology and was responsible for organising the first museums in France.

The former **St. Vincent's Cathedral** brings together a variety of architectural styles ranging from Romanesque to Neo-Gothic (West Front and towers). The cloisters are particularly tranquil. The 15th-century **Doyenné Tower**, once part of a house in Old Chalon, was taken to pieces in 1907,

carried off to Paris, and purchased by Frank Jay Gould who rebuilt it and gave it back to the people of Chalon in 1928.

The **Côte Chalonnaise Wine Office** (tasting, shop, restaurant) is in the attractive Fair Chalet on the Promenade Sainte-Marie (closed Sundays and Mondays). The **Côte chalonnaise vineyards** (Rully, Mercurey, Montagny and Givry) are close by.

TOURNUS

This "piece of music in stone" as it was described by Christian Doumet is the abbey church of **Saint-Philibert de Tournus,** a masterpiece of Burgundian Romanesque architecture dedicated to two saints - Valérien and Philibert whose remains worked miracles until the 17th century.

St.Valérien was beheaded in Tournus in 179 A.D. His tomb aroused great fervour and he became a cult figure. There was already a church on this site in the 6th century, according to St. Gregory of Tours and an abbey was established later. A religious community from Noirmoutier, who had been forced out of its own monastery by the Viking invasions, had wandered right across the country with the relics of St.Philibert before arriving in Tournus in 875 A.D. The monastery remained independent despite the close proximity of Cluny, and it applied the Rule of St.Benedict. But the two saints, Valérien and Philibert, are not always a well-matched couple - one had to be put in the crypt and the other in the upper church.

Between the 9th and 17th centuries, the abbey gradually built up considerable temporal power throughout the region. Its buildings were reconstructed in the late 10th century by Abbot Etienne, in the style of Clermont cathedral (**crypt**) but with marked Italian (or Lombard) influences and features reminiscent of Auvergne and the Poitiers area. The **narthex** probably dates from this period. After a fire in 1007, Abbot Bernier had the nave rebuilt, possibly with the help of masons from Ravenna. The new church was completed in 1019. The work continued under Abbot Pierre I and his successor, Francon du Rouzay. Was there a certain Spanish influence? The pink and white voussoirs on the ribbed arches bear a resemblance to the mosque in Cordoba... The decoration of the chancel and transept probably dates from the 12th century and Romanesque imagination was left to run riot - on one capital there is a devil pulling out the tongue of a scandalmonger. In St.Michael's

The interior of St.Philibert's.

Chapel is the strange figure of Gerlannus, in a style similar to Carolingian art. The square belltower above the apse dates from the 12th century.

A visit to St.Philibert's today ends with the **chapter house** (13th century) and **abbot's lodgings** (15th century). The organ was built in the 17th century and has a "swallow's nest" organ-chest. **Notre-Dame-la-Brune** (the Brown Virgin) is a 12th-century cedarwood statue of the Virgin Mary in the Byzantine style.

Tournus was badly damaged by the Calvinists in 1562. The abbey fell into a decline and was "secularised" in 1627 - the monks were replaced by canons. Cardinal de Bouillon and Cardinal de Fleury were both abbots of Tournus. The decorative features they commissioned did little to ornament the building. The abbey died a fine death in 1785 and its income was shared out between the bishoprics of Chalon-sur-Saône and Mâcon and the chapter of Neuville-les-Dames. The Revolution dealt the institution a further blow. Yet the buildings were saved and were classified as historic monuments in 1841. Restora-

The north gallery, all that remains of the cloister.

tion was undertaken by Questel between 1946 and 1951. The distemper that had covered the inside walls since the days of Cardinal de Fleury was removed between 1905 and 1910 and the church regained its original pink tinge (from the Préty building stone). The stained glass windows were partially smashed when the bridge over the R.Saône was blown up in 1940 and 1944. They were rebuilt by Brigitte Simon.

The **Greuze Museum** is in the former Benedictine Convent (18th century) : archaeological finds from the Tournus area and mediaeval exhibits, oriental pieces, work by the primitives, paintings by J.B.Greuze and Félix Ziem. Greuze deserves more than the reputation of a rather mawkish artist that unfortunately still clings to him (open to the public daily except Tuesdays and Sunday mornings).

The **Perrin-de-Puycousin Museum** in the family home of Albert Thibaudet (17th century) is also worth a visit. Maurice Perrin de Puycousin was a barrister, born in Tournus in 1856 ; he died in 1949. He was particularly interested in the folklore of Burgundy and Bresse. At that time, he was something of a pioneer in France. His collections were used as the basis of two museums - in Tournus in 1929 and in Dijon in 1938. Fascinating forerunners of the present-day museums of popular arts and traditions.

The narthex.

Top : The village of Brancion.

The superb Romanesque church in Chapaize. ▶

BRANCION

A spot with plenty of character and charm : old covered market and old houses, a pleasant village that abounds with flowers, a 13th-century **church** (early 14th-century frescoes) and the tomb of one of St.Louis' companions, the Lord of Brancion, who was killed at the Battle of Mansourah (1250) during the Crusades.

The castle stands in **Martailly-lès-Brancion**. First built in the days of the Ancient Burgundians and fortified in the 10th century, it was a veritable eagle's nest for the mighty Brancion family who maintained a constant feud with Cluny. The castle then passed to the Dukes of Burgundy and, later, to the King. It was described as "one of the key positions in the country". It put up fierce resistance during the League (Saulx-Tavannes).

In **Chapaize** there is a superb late 10th-century church and the remains of **Lancharre Abbey**.

The north wall and pepper-pot towers of Cormatin.

Overleaf : Cluny : the former cellar with ribbed vaulting, in the flour store.

CORMATIN (Château)

Yet another château being given a new lease of life ! Built in the early years of the 17th century on an island in the Grosne, it was originally commissioned by Antoine Du Blé d'Uxelles, Governor of Chalon. In 1730, on the death of the Maréchal d'Uxelles, President of the Council of Foreign Affairs during the Regency, it passed into other hands. In particular, it belonged for a time to Pierre Dezoteux who took part in the American War of Independence and, later, in the Royalist, or "Chouan" Revolt under the name of "Baron de Cormatin".

Some years later, the Château de Cormatin entered the literary scene. Nina Dezoteux, wife of Guillaume de Pierreclau and a childhood friend of Alphonse de Lamartine, fell in love with the poet and had a son by him in 1813, Léon de Pierreclau.

The author Jacques de Lacretelle was born here in 1888. At the turn of the century, the château's owner invited all the top celebrities of the day to stay at Cormatin - Cécile Sorel, Chaliapine, Diaghilev, Saint-Saëns, Fauré, Massenet etc. The owner was, of course, Raoul Guns-bourg, Director of the Monte-Carlo Opera, and the "inventor" of the Great Caruso.

In 1981, four enthusiastic friends began to save Cormatin, starting with the restoration of the "gilded apartments" (one of the most sumptuous interiors from the reign of Louis XIII anywhere in France), the laying out of the courtyards as they were in the 17th century, the opening up of the fourth side of the building, the redesigning of the gardens as they were in the 17th century, reroofing, etc.

TAIZE

This new mystical Burgundian hill has worldwide influence. Yet Taizé is better-known abroad than in France itself. It is a spiritual grafting operation, with Burgundy providing the venture with its skies, its scenery, and its setting.

Roger Schutz was the son of a Swiss Protestant pastor and his Burgundian wife and he studied theology in Lausanne. In 1940, he thought about opening a home in Burgundy for men who had lost all hope in the future - "a place of silence and work". Quite by chance, he discovered that there was an estate for sale in Taizé. And this is how the "Cluny community" was born, in Lausanne. In autumn 1944, Roger Schutz and three Swiss friends settled in Taizé. The oecumenical community gradually expanded, opening its doors to Protestant, Roman Catholic and Anglican brothers. In 1949, the annual promise to live as a community became a lifelong undertaking when Roger Schutz wrote the Rule of Taizé.

In 1948, the community received permission to use the Romanesque church in the village for its services and three daily prayers. Then there came the Church of Reconciliation, built on the plateau.

Taizé played an active part in the Vatican II Council. The community set up numerous links with the Third World. On 30th August 1974, the Council of Youth was opened in Taizé, in the presence of 40,000 participants from all over the world. Its sessions continue from year to year. Pope Jean-Paul II visited Taizé in 1986.

An ambiguous venture, without any doubt. Yet nowhere else in Europe is there a sacred place that spontaneously draws in so many young people.

When there are meetings and assemblies, Taizé is one huge hive of discussion. During the remainder of the year, it is a secret spot. Don't forget to visit the two churches in the village. A shop sells works published by the community and by individual brothers. Brother Roger is rarely in Taizé.

CLUNY

Cluny Abbey, a focal point for the Christian world, has almost entirely disappeared. Because of demolition work during the Revolution ? Not a bit of it. Because of senseless vandalism c.1820. In order to get the stone, the abbey church was blown up, bringing the wonderful capitals down to earth with a bump.

All that remain of the abbey today are the Holy Water Tower, the south transept crossing of the church, a few chapels, a few ruins, the odd capital or two, and a few carved stones (open to the public, closed Tuesdays).

Founded in 910 A.D. in the valley of the Grosne, a river that wends its sleepy way from Beaujolais to Saône, Cluny Abbey owed its being to a donation from the Duke of Aquitaine, William the Pious, and to the efforts of Bernon, Abbot of Baume-les-Messieurs in Jura and Mouthier-en-Bresse. It was a Benedictine abbey and it restored the Rule of St.Benedict (6th century). It was fortunate to have a whole succession of outstanding abbots, the "Saints of Cluny". In addition to Bernon who placed the monastery under the direct jurisdiction of the Pope, thereby ensuring a large measure of independence vis-à-vis the local temporal powers, there was Odo (who could make his monks laugh till tears poured down their faces), Mayeul (who refused to become Pope), Odilon (who instituted the Feast of All Saints), and Hugh (who encouraged the Holy Roman Emperor, Henry IV, to travel to Canossa to be reconciled with the Pope). And all this between 1000 A.D. and 1100 A.D.

Cluny soon found itself at the head of 1,200 monasteries or priories, in Europe and the Holy Land. The supreme authority of the abbot of Cluny gave him the same status as an emperor in Europe. His loyalty to the Pope strengthened the influence of Rome. The Black Monks' order was beginning to fall into decline when St.Bernard sought to establish a new purity in Cîteaux and, later, in Clairvaux. The White Monks took over from their predecessors.

The transept and south tower, all that remains of the once huge abbey church. ▶

The upper room in the flour store.

The Fabry Tower. ▶

But Cluny was an empire. "Wherever the wind blows, the Abbot of Cluny gets income" says a Burgundian proverb. Popes Gregory VII, Urban II and Paschal II all rose from this Order.

The **third church in Cluny** was commissioned by the future St.Hugh and built in 1088 and 1130. It was the largest building in the Christian world until St.Peter's was built in Rome - a truly gigantic construction - 608 ft. long, vaulting 98 ft. high, 162-foot towers, and 12,000 cubic meters of rubble buried underneath to provide foundations for the chancel. It was, though, a graceful building because of the systematic use of ribbed and barrel vaulting, the inclusion of Gothic features, and the enthusiasm which soon communicated itself to people throughout Burgundy. A Romanesque building but with an all-pervading sense of verticality. The American archaeologist Kenneth J. Conant, who died in 1984, gave his whole life to the recreation of the abbey, a "canticle in stone" built to a carefully thought-out plan. In days gone by, people spoke of the "angels' walkway" and the "Promised Land" when they came face to face with the abbey in all its splendour.

The Cluny School of Arts and Crafts was set up in a part of the 18th-century buildings.

Abélard's limetree (23 ft. in circumference) is said to be as old as the famous theologian, the unhappy lover of Héloïse, whom Peter the Venerable took into Cluny in 1140 after his differences of opinion with St.Bernard.

Visitors can still see the **Flour Store** (13th century) and the 12th-century **Milltower.** Capitals and models in the **former cellar.** From the **Cheese Tower** (11th and 12th centuries) there is an interesting

panoramic view of the town. The **Ochier Museum** is in the former Abbot's Palace (15th century) and it includes a room of archaeological exhibits and a fine library (closed 20th December to 15th January). The town hall is housed in the former **Amboise Mansion.** Note, too, the **Fabry Tower** (14th century).

The **Cluny Stud** is one of the breeding stations created in 1806 to bring breeding stock together in one place. It was at this time that the Charolais horse acquired its reputation. This stud, the only one in Burgundy, still fulfils its original purpose, with just over one hundred stallions - thoroughbreds, French trotters, Anglo-Arab stock, poneys, Ardennais, Percherons and Comtois... Every year, four to five thousand mares are covered by these precious stallions. Among the stars that began life in Cluny was Bellino II who won the America Cup three times (1975-1977). Open to the public but the stallions are ''at work'' away from the stud from February to July.

7 miles from Cluny are the **Azé Caves and Blanot Swallowhole,** a gash in the ground some 260 ft. deep (21 chambers. Open to the public March - October.

In **Mazille,** the Carmelite Convent of Peace was designed by J.L. Sert in 1971. The community has just over thirty nuns and is a recent order of ''Theresian'' sisters from Châlons-sur-Marne.

◀ The Pope Gelase façade, restored during last century.

The Holy Water Tower in Cluny. ▶

"Milly, the homeland", a painting by Jean Laronze (Lamartine Museum, Mâcon).

The tiny Romanesque church of Saint-Point. ▶

LAMARTINE COUNTRY

"There my heart in every place finds itself,

I am remembered, known, loved by everything ..."

Alphonse de Lamartine had countless connections with the Mâcon region. The literary pilgrimage begins in **Mâcon** where Lamartine was born in 1790, in the outhouses of the family mansion on the Rue Bauderon de Senecé. In the Rue Lamartine, the child lived in the Ozenay Mansion, which his father purchased in 1805. In the Rue Sigorgne, there is a museum housing memorabilia (Senecé Mansion).

In Prissé is the **Château de Monceau** built in 1648. The Lamartines purchased it in 1662 and the poet inherited it in 1834. He lived there on his return from the Far East. Part of his History of the Girondists was written here. The Ode to the Comte d'Orsay was penned in Montceau. The Academy of Mâcon owns and maintains the small octagonal pavilion in the midst of the vineyard to which Lamartine came on numerous occasions. The château belongs to the Ozanam Foundation.

Ah, Milly ! Remember the famous lines :

"On the deformed threshold of three stone steps

Chance planted the roots of an ivy...

... There is the rustic bench where once sat my father

The chamber where rang out his strict masculine voice..."

Built in 1705, the house in Milly was lived in by Alphonse de Lamartine's father in 1794. For the poet, this will always be a place filled with family memories. Yet he sold it in 1860, when being sued for debt, writing as he did so this poignant cry of farewell, *La Vigne et la Maison*.

"The soul in despair finds sad charms.." Michelet wrote to him, "Your words set me weeping".

Bussières is the background to *Jocelyn*; it is the village where Lamartine was educated as a child, by the local priest. At that time, his teacher was Father Dumont. The poem *Jocelyn* (1836) retraces the life of a priest and is based on the story of Father Dumont, who fell in love with Jacqueline de Pierreclau during

the Revolution but who later came back into the Church. His gravestone stands against the sacristy and the epitaph was written by Lamartine.

Jacqueline de Pierreclau (renamed Laurence by Lamartine) lived in the **Chateau de Pierreclos** (keep and main building dating from 11th and 12th centuries). Lamartine was friendly with Guillaume de Pierreclau and had an affair with his wife, Nina de Pierreclau, by whom he had a son.

Finally, **Saint-Point** (museum). In 1802, Lamartine's father purchased this old feudal manorhouse. The poet was given it in 1820. He had the château altered in the "troubadour Gothic" style of the times and had a keep, gallery, and crenelations added. Lamartine made frequent visits to Saint-Point, which was his favourite house. It was here that he wrote *Jocelyn, La Chute d'un Ange* etc. He is buried here and visitors can almost imagine him continuing his discussion with the Stonecutter of Saint-Point...

The château now belongs to the Noblet d'Anglure family, who is descended from one of the poet's sisters. In 1840, Lamartine wrote :

"This is why the vine interwoven
With memories of my childhood
Brings a thought to my soul
And has to twist its way over my grave."

Because of these lines, the Academy of Mâcon planted a vine at the foot of the grave in Saint-Point in 1940.

The route through Lamartine country is also a Wine Route (Igé, La Roche Vineuse etc.)

Lamartine's home in Saint-Point.

The Solutré Rock.

SOLUTRE

In 1869, Solutré gave its name to a period of prehistory, the Solutrean, which lies between the Perigordian-Aurignacian and the Magdalanian (Early Paleolithic c.20,000 years B.C.). The limestone outcrop juts up unexpectedly out of the orderly Mâcon countryside. At the top is a narrow plateau at an altitude of over 1,000 feet. Then there is a sheer drop of 97 ft. to 130 ft. On the rockfalls and in the shelter of the vertical walls is the **Crôt du Charnier prehistoric centre.** Research began in 1866 with Adrien Arcelin and Henri de Ferry. It was continued by Father Breuil in 1907, in the 20's by the universities in the Lyons area etc.

There was a settlement here c.35,000 B.C. (Mousterian Age). Remains show that it then provided shelter for an advanced civilisation 15,000 years later. This was Cro-Magnon Man who hunted with mechanically-propelled spears, used needles for sewing and decorated clothing with jewellery and necklaces.

of almost 4 hectares to a depth of sometimes as much as 6 ft. 6 ins. Specialists believe this was a graveyard for between 10,000 and 100,000 horses. Were they frightened and did they leap to their deaths off the top of the rock? Or were they killed by this hunter people, when the flocks and herds were moving from the Sâone Plain to the hinterland? Prehistorians are divided on this point, but all of them agree that the events took place in the Perigordian Age (30,000 to 22,000 B.C.). The Solutré horse stood 4 ft. 7 ins. high.

Experts have also uncovered a mammoth and deer carved in the round.

Later, the Solutreans became great artists in hewn stone. They used flint to make superb spear heads called "laurel leaves" using a process that involved peeling off thin "slices" of flint.

The village of Vergisson.

In addition to this remarkable Stone Age industry (the finest Solutrean objects were discovered in 1874 in Volgu between Gueugnon and Digoin and are now on show in the museum in Chalon-sur-Sâone), the famous "horse magma" was also found here - a **pile of horse bones** welded together and covering an area

▲ The Pouilly-Fuissé vineyard.

Every year since 1946, François Mitterand has spent Whitsunday climbing the Solutré Rock. In October 1944, he married a young girl from Cluny called Danielle Gouze.

The **Museum** was inaugurated in 1987.

With Fuissé, Chaintré, and Vergisson, Solutré is one of the four parishes that produce the excellent Pouilly-Fuissé, a white burgundy from the Chardonnay grape.

◀ Another view of the Solutré Rock.

Mâcon old town.

Overleaf : The houses along the Quai Lamartine on the banks of the R.Saône.

MACON

Mâcon is both the "Queen of the Sâone" and Lamartine's town.

The river is peaceful, except when it bursts its banks (in days gone by, a child who wet the bed was said to have "done a Sâone"). Normally, it is 4 ft. 9 ins. deep. Since 1640, there have been 15 floods with the river running at a depth of 20 ft. and most of the streets under water.

Across the river is the **St.Lawrence Bridge.** For the local people, it is the apple of their eye. It is an 11th-century construction, fortified in the 14th century, and rebuilt in 1772 and again in 1843 to meet the needs of steam-powered river traffic.

As for Alphonse de Lamartine (1790-1869) he is to be found everywhere in Mâcon. His **birthplace** is in the Rue des Ursulines. The **Senecé**

Mansion (Regency, built between 1710 and 1748) has been the seat of the Academy of Mâcon since 1795 and is now a Lamartine Study Centre. The **statue** of the great man stands on the riverbank (by Alexandre Falguière, 1875). There is even a mural depicting the Mâcon banquet (1847) in honour of Lamartine's speech as a left-wing opponent of the July monarchy. The mural is on a block of renovated council flats in the Rue Edouard-Herriot.

Mâcon is a very old town, a frontier community until 1601 but always with decided leanings towards France. St.Louis purchased the Mâconnais region in 1239 from the last Comte Jean de Braine. The county became the property of the Duke of Burgundy (1435) before

being annexed to the Crown again in 1477. But Mâcon was careful to retain its own "special characteristics". With the French Revolution, it became a county town despite strong rivalry with Chalon-sur-Sâone.

A visit to Mâcon starts on the **quays** with their 18th- and 19th-century houses. They are bright and lively. Opposite Lamartine's statue, the **town hall** is housed in the former Comte de Montrevel's residence (1750). The former **Charity Hospice** (chapel) was designed by Soufflot (1752-1762). The **Timbered House** (1500) on the Place aux Herbes has some extraordinary decorative features. **"Old St. Vincent's"** has suffered a lot of damage. Poor cathedral... The new St.Vincent's Church,

105

The St.Lawrence Bridge and the two ▲ strange tower of "Old St.Vincent's".

A mural painted in 1983 showing Lamartine as "part of the left-wing ▶ opposition".

built thanks to a donation from Napoleon, was called in turn St.Napoleon's, St.Louis' (during the Restoration of the Monarchy) and St.Vincent's in homage to the patron saint of wine-growers. The **Hospital** was built in 1761 and was also designed by Soufflot (dome, dispensary).

The **Ursuline Museum** (closed Tuesdays) in a 17th-century convent that later became a prison and barracks is also worth a visit. The collections include references to Solutré, of course, as well as to the Gallo-Roman period and to the Saône's boatmen.

The **Lamartine Museum** (open May-Sept.) is housed in the Senecé Mansion - there are exhibits relating to the writer and statesman as well as furniture, tapestries etc.

A fresco in the chancel of the church in Anzy-le-Duc.

ANZY-LE-DUC

The church in Anzy-le-Duc is a perfect illustration of Romanesque architecture in the Brionnais region (11th and 12th centuries). Capitals, Romanesque frescoes, and a superb octagonal three-storey belltower. It is said to have provided inspiration for the builders of Vézelay.

Apart from one doorway, it is all that remains of the old priory in Anzy-le-Duc.

The Brionnais region, which was once a bailiwick of the Duchy of Burgundy, has maintained its vocation as a producer of Charolais cattle. There are numerous churches in the Cluny style, like the one in **Montceaux-l'Etoile** (early 12th-century doorway illustrating the Ascension, the usual theme on the tympana in this area).

Lower down on the map are **Marcigny**, which is already getting near Roanne (old houses, 18th-century Cudel de Montcolon mansion, Mill

The tympanum on the West Front of the church in Anzy-le-Duc.

tower now a small local museum) and **Semur-en-Brionnais** (Château Saint-Hugues, birthplace of one of the earliest abbots of Cluny, 12th- and 13th-century church, 18th-century town hall). In **Ligny-en-Brionnais,** there is a former Benedictine abbey (St.Rigaud's) where Peter the Hermit preached the first Crusade.

In the same area are a number of interesting churches - **Iguerande, Perrecy-les-Forges** (formerly dependent on the abbey of Saint-Benoît-sur-Loire), **Saint-Germain-en-Brionnais, Bois-Sainte-Marie,** etc. In **Saint-Christophe-en-Brionnais,** there is a **cattle market** every Thursday morning.

◄ Anzy-le-Duc, the wonderful Romanesque belltower.

The tympanum on the church of Montceau-l'Etoile.

Perrecy-les-Forges, general view and south aisle.

The superb chevet on the church in Semur-en-Brionnais.

PARAY-LE-MONIAL

The holy town of Burgundy, Paray-le-Monial, was the originator of **devotion to the Sacred Heart.**

Marguerite-Marie Alacoque entered the Convent of the Visitation in Paray-le-Monial in 1671. She had four visions during which Christ revealed the Sacred Heart to her (1673-1676). But the nun met with scepticism and hostility before her mission was finally accomplished. Marguerite-Marie Alacoque died in 1690 at the age of 43, was beatified in 1864 and canonised in 1920 by Pope Benedict XV. Her Saint's Day is October 17th, the anniversary of her death. Her councillor and friend, Father Claude de la Colombière was canonised in 1992. It was he who spread word of the young Visitandine's visions.

It was in the convent in Paray-le-Monial that the Sacred Heart became the object of worship for the first time, in 1686. Marseilles was dedicated to the Sacred Heart in 1722 and, in 1794, the revolt in Vendée took the Heart as its emblem. Devotion spread widely throughout the 19th century. After the Franco-Prussian War in 1870, the National Vow Committee undertook to gather sufficient money to build the Sacré Coeur in Montmartre; it was completed in 1919. Paray-le-Monial was the setting for the first great national pilgrimage, held in 1873. In 1899, Pope Leo XIII declared the devotion of the human species to the Sacred Heart. A college of chaplains organises the **pilgrimages** which bring 200,000 to 400,000 people to the town every year. Since 1975, there have also been meetings of the Charismatic Revival.

The **minster,** which was elevated to the rank of minor basilica in 1875 and given the name Sacred Heart (Sacré Coeur), stands near the R. Bourbince. Built between 1090 and 1110 as a copy of the third of Cluny's churches, it has all the perfection of a masterpiece - the presence of light and a discreet ornamentation. "It tells us what happens in heaven", wrote Canon Denis Grivot. Pope John Paul II celebrated Mass in

The ambulatory in the abbey church.

Paray-le-Monial on 5th October 1986.

Memorabilia relating to St.Marguerite-Marie are exhibited in the **Chamber of Relics** in the former palace of the Abbot of Cluny. The slide show was designed in 1935 by Georges Serraz. **Chaplains' Park** where the processions take place is worth a visit. **The Chapel of the Visi-**

tation where the saint experienced her visions now contains her reliquary in silver gilt (stained glass windows and painting by Luc Barbier). The **Le Hiéron Eucharistic Museum** (1890) houses not only numerous religious and liturgical items but also the magnificent tympanum from the Benedictine abbey of Anzy-le-Duc (11th century). The basilica and Chapel of the Visitation are open daily until 7 p.m. Museums open May to September.

The town hall occupies the amazing **Renaissance House** built in 1525 for a cloth merchant named Pierre Jayet. The façade with its 26 medallions of the kings of France etc. has some extraordinary decorative features.

The **Brotherhood of the Free Cacous**, which was founded in 1972, holds a chapter every year when the cherries are ripe. The ''Cacou'' is a milk pudding containing unstoned cherries, one of the local specialities. Hence the nickname of ''Cacous'' given to the people of Paray. They even have an imaginary ancestor called Jean-Marie Cacou, a much less austere figure than Marguerite-Marie...

◀ The Renaissance mansion that now houses the town hall.

Top : A 14th-century fresco in the barrel-vaulted apse.

The Basilica of the Sacred Heart. ▶

NEVERS

Do you remember *Hiroshima my love*? The timeless town in Alain Resnais' film based on a story by Marguerite Duras was Nevers.

It is neither typically Burgundian nor even Nivernais; Nevers is a Loire Valley town with certain characteristics reminiscent of the Bourbonnais and Berry regions. It had been a Eduen settlement before being annexed to the Senones province by the Romans and, later, being the home of the Ancient Burgundians (502 A.D.). Its prosperity resulted in the presence of a bishopric. It was granted a charter in 1164. The bell towers and turrets are so close together that it is described as the "pointed town".

In 1184, Pierre de Courtenay became the first Count of Nevers to show any interest in his town. He had new ramparts built. John Lackland received the title of Comte de Nevers from his father and the region was part of the House of Burgundy before becoming Rhenish with the arrival of the Cleves. Raised to a duchy and peerage in 1538, the Nevers region reached the climax of its prosperity and influence in the days of the Gonzague family who had come from Mantua in the 16th century as the result of a marriage.

Mazarin purchased the Nivernais region in 1659. The Mancinis were its last dukes, right up to the time of the Revolution. Fouché was already in place, ready to govern the newly-created *département* (or county) that had Nevers as its main town. He gave the daughter born to him during his stay in the region the gently-sounding forename, Nièvre.

In the 18th century, Nevers had highly profitable industries on its doorstep. The forests, river and iron ore led to the opening of numerous forges nearby - **Imphy, Guérigny, Fourchambault,** all of them to fall into a gradual decline.

The chevet of St.Stephen's Church.

117

Nevers glazed earthenware (photo by Francis Morin).

The Croux Gate. ▶

The town is especially rich in reminders of the two great periods in its history - the first one stretching from the Middle Ages to the Renaissance and the other one covering the 19th-century Industrial Revolution. During the night of 16th-17th July 1944, the R.A.F. launched 108 bombers on Nevers in order to block the German retreat by destroying the railway junction. But the 1,200 bombs that were dropped spread far afield. The tragedy caused 162 deaths, and destroyed or seriously damaged 500 blocks of flats.

The **Crous Gateway** is a reminder of the 12th-century wall. It is a fine example of 14th-century defensive architecture and its guardroom houses a **small archaeological museum** (collections from Antiquity and Romanesque period). The **Goguin Tower** (1419) was originally a windmill. The **St.Ely Tower** dates from 1421. The **Paris Gate** is proof of the homage paid to Louis XV by the people of Nevers after the Battle of Fontenoy.

The **Ducal Palace,** which was designed to replace the former Courtenay Castle, was built in 1460 for Jean de Clamecy. Although basically a mediaeval construction (large towers on the sides, tall round chimneys, steeply-sloping roofs), the Cleves and Gonzague families gave it a more Italianate Renaissance touch (note the elegant façade). The ducal palace was the first of the Loire Valley castles and it has a wealth of decorative features. It looks onto a vast esplanade. The view was the brainchild of Charles de Gonzague.

The **cathedral of St.Cyr and St.Julitte** was built in the 12th and 13th centuries over a 6th-century baptistery. The chancel was rebuilt in the 14th century. The church has two apses - the Romanesque one is an incitement to meditation and the Gothic one serves to elevate the spirit. Its square tower is 169 ft. high. It was badly damaged by the 1944 air raid but restoration work was completed in 1967. The stained glass was commissioned from Pierre Soulages, Sam Francis and Simon Hantaï in 1984. **St.Stephen's** (Saint-Etienne), which dates from the late 11th century, indicates the influence of Cluny. The former chapel of the Jesuit college, St. Peter's (Saint-Pierre), makes no attempt to hide its Louis XIII origins (it houses a painting by Le Nain). The Baroque **St.Mary's Chapel** was once the sanctuary in the Convent of the Visitation. The Church of St.Bernadette du Banlay (20th century) was designed by the architect Claude Parent.

The Arts Centre was built in the 1960's and stands out rather like a

◄ The Gothic nave in the cathedral.

wart on the banks of the Loire. The Jean-Jaurès Cultural Centre (library and college of music) is another piece of contemporary architecture.

Nevers' famous people have nearly all been women - Henrietta of Cleves, wife of Louis de Gonzague; Marie de Gonzague who became Queen of Poland by marrying Ladislas IV and, later, his brother and successor Jean Casimir; her goddaughter and follower Marie de la Grange d'Arquian who married Jean Sobieski and was also Queen of Poland; and **Bernadette Soubirous** who entered the Convent of the Sisters of Nevers in Lourdes where she remained for 8 years before being admitted to the mother house. She took the veil here in 1866 under the name of Sister Marie-Bernard. She worked in the infirmary where she led a discreet life. She died in 1879 at the age of 36. She was buried in the **Chapel of the Convent of St. Gildard of Nevers** where her body lies on view in a reliquary. St. Bernadette of Lourdes was beatified in 1925 and canonised in 1933 by Pius X (museum).

While in Nevers, remember to try the famous **négus** and **abyssin**. In addition to the nougatine, honey "caraques", and "roseaux", the town offers sweet-lovers a soft chocolate caramel covered in a hard sugar coating that was christened "négus" when the Negus of Abyssinia, Menelik, visited France in 1902. The "abyssin" is coffee-flavoured and slightly lighter in colour (buy them at the Confiserie Lyron, 96 rue du Commerce, which, like the Maison Fourgnal at 75 rue du Commerce, is worth a visit for its wonderfully preserved 19th-century commercial architecture).

Nevers holds some rather unusual records of birth - the **Charolais Herdbook** which includes details of some 200,000 animals and their family trees (updated by computer). The herdbook is designed to maintain the essential characteristics of this top-class breed of cattle.

Yet, as Marie-Claude Pascal wrote, "Nevers' glory lies in its gla-

The square tower on the cathedral.

Overleaf : The Duke's Palace.

zed earthenware". It appeared in the town in the 16th century, the heyday of the Court of the Gonzagues. An Italian named Augustin Conrade from Savona created a style using a range of blues enhanced by manganese-based purple motifs. Julio Gambin joined him. Then the Custodes strengthened the hold of an art form that was purely Nivernais, the famous "**Nevers blue**". The

great creative period ran from 1630 to 1730 and there were numerous workshops (12 in the 18th century, employing 1,500 people). The only one that still exists is the Bout du Monde. The **Municipal Museum** (16 Rue Saint-Genest) shows the evolution of this craft - the Italian tradition, items with grained bases, Persian designs, and items dating from the Revolution.

The tympanum moved from the Holy Cross Tower to the south arm of the transept in the church.

The old bridge, with the Holy Cross Tower in the background. ▶

LA CHARITE-SUR-LOIRE

As the daughter of Cluny in the mid 11th century and the mother of some fifty other daughter-houses in France and abroad (the furthest being near Constantinople), La Charité was once "one of the wonders of Europe", as Denis Grivot described it. It lay on the road to Compostella (pilgrims coming from Vézelay crossed the R. Loire here) and the **abbey** (or, to be more precise, the priory) that was the eldest of Cluny's five daughters was exceedingly prosperous in the 12th century. Moreover, it enjoyed such a fine reputation that it was given the name of the first of the three theological virtues. "Going to Charity" became a common expression in the neighbourhood,

and paupers and pilgrims alike came here in large numbers to receive alms from the good fathers. The abbey's coat-of-arms was eloquent indeed - three open purses!

La Charité, the "Princess of the Loire", has slate roofs huddling round the tower of a **priory church** that was consecrated in 1107 by Pope Paschal II. Devastated by fire in 1559, the church had originally been as vast as the gigantic minster in Cluny. Poor St.Bernard! The striking decorative features on its West Front are in total contrast to his ideas... It looks rather like a stocklist of everything in the 12th-century imagination. Note the **tympanum** illustrating the arrival of the Virgin Mary in Heaven. There is a second **tympanum**, inside the church. The

tops of the pillars are decorated with a veritable menagerie of Romanesque creatures - dragons, mermaids, basilisks, dromadaries, lions, monkeys, salamanders, snakes etc. The nave was rebuilt in the late 17th century. It is 397 ft. long, 88 ft. high and 120 ft. wide and the church could take 5,000 pilgrims. Is this still the "temple of Beauty" described by Victor Hugo? The restoration work on the building is sometimes too obvious but at least the church has been saved. Prosper Mérimée ensured that the projected Paris-Nevers road was never built because it was supposed to pass through the middle of the abbey. The tympanum that is still in its original position was invisible until 1923 when a house blocking it up was finally demolished.

In 1975, another architectural gem was brought to light - the chancel of one of the monastery's original churches dating from the first half of the 11th century. It may have been built over a Carolingian building (painted decoration and carvings, tiling). Digs are currently underway.

Franciscan Convent (open to the public except during winter). **Museum** (July and August) : earthenware, local folklore collections.

The map on pages 2-3 was drawn by Christophe Chauvin.

INDEX

Cet ouvrage a été imprimé par l'Imprimerie Pollina S.A. à Luçon (85) - n° 15804
I.S.B.N. 2.7373.0200.5 - Dépôt légal : juin 1988
N° éditeur : 1513.04.03.02.93